DON'T

Unlock the *do* in *don't*...

HOW USING THE RIGHT WORDS WILL CHANGE YOUR LIFE

Bob Selden
PO Box 8
Ashhurst, Palmerston North, 4470
New Zealand
ISBN 978-0-9944508-0-7

Copyright © Bob Selden 2022
This book is copyright. Apart from any fair dealing for the purposes of private study, research, criticism or review permitted under the Copyright Act 1968, no part may be stored or reproduced by any process without prior written permission.

Enquiries should be made to the author, Bob Selden. www.bobselden.com

The author has performed in good faith, a diligent search to identify and locate the owner of all work quoted in this book before publication. The author has endeavoured to reference any work quoted in this book to the original owner and where appropriate and/or extensive, contacted same for their approval.

National Library of Australia
Cataloguing-in-publication data:
Creator: Selden, Bob, author.
Title: Don't: how using the right words will change your life / Bob Selden.

ISBN: 978-0-6454956-0-7 (paperback)

Notes: Includes bibliographical references and index.

Subjects:
  Positivism.
  Thought and thinking.
  Self-actualization (Psychology).
  Behaviour modification.
  Interpersonal communication.
  Conduct of life.

Dewey Number: 153.42

Cover design by: Alli Spoor
Internals designed and typeset by Mercier Typesetters Pty Ltd, Telopea, NSW
www.merciers.com.au
Distributed by Ingram Spark

Unlock the *do* in *don't*...

HOW USING THE RIGHT WORDS WILL CHANGE YOUR LIFE

BOB SELDEN

CONTENTS

Introduction ix

PART ONE
How words impact our behaviour

Chapter 1: **Impact of the word 'don't'**

Can you actually influence the behaviour of others? 3

Chapter 2: **Choose the best words – become more positive**

Can certain words we regularly use affect our own behaviour? 15

Chapter 3: **What impact does our 'personal' language have on our behaviour?**

Can words affect how much you save? How much you eat? How much safe sex you have? 27

Chapter 4: **Metaphors and the use of 'and'**

How clean is our language? 34

Chapter 5: **How to use words, metaphors and actions to affect your feelings**

Can what we say influence how we feel? 45

Chapter 6: **How positive and negative words affect brain power**

Can the words we use change the way our brain functions? 56

PART TWO
Words to use, words to avoid and other influencing factors when communicating

Chapter 7: Words or phrases which make difficult conversations even more difficult
Can words make or break a relationship? 65

Chapter 8: The importance of tone of voice
Can words alone ensure our message has the desired impact? 85

Chapter 9: The process of a conversation
Can you actively manage a conversation? 93

PART THREE
Difficult conversations and how to manage these

Chapter 10: Spouse to spouse, or partner to partner
"We need to talk" 124

Chapter 11: Parent conversation with a young adult
How can you engage, really engage, with your son or daughter? 135

Chapter 12: Teenage conversation with parents
How can you talk about really difficult subjects with Mum and Dad? 145

Chapter 13: Conversation with an ageing parent
A heart-to-heart discussion 153

Chapter 14: Giving ~~critical~~ *favourable* feedback to a friend
How can you give someone news they may not like and still remain friends? 164

CONTENTS

Chapter 15: The conversation you're having when you're not having a conversation
How to get what you want, really get what you want 178

Chapter 16: Creating an image – can a speech do it?
How to build word pictures that resonate with your audience 190

Chapter 17: When does a conversation become a negotiation?
Tips to improve success in all negotiations 206

Chapter 18: Conversation titbits
How to overcome conversation stoppers and improve conversation deepeners 217

Conclusion 232

Suggested answers to the short exercises contained in Chapters 1, 2 & 7 236

Acknowledgements 241

References 244

Index 253

Introduction:
Are you Positive or Negative?

Does your behaviour impact those around you – and can you change it?

Some years ago in the sports section of my local newspaper I read a report by Spiro Zavos which described the behaviour of a football coach during a very tense finals game. The antics of the losing coach gave a clear insight into why his team did not win and in fact why it continues to lose many close games.

In part, Zavos' report read:

"He was at his over-emotional worst at Lancaster Park on Sunday. The eyes rolled more wildly than ever, he stalked the sideline. Not even the television cameras were safe from his flaying arms. His antics sent a damaging message to his team; that the fates are conspiring against them and they are, somehow, destined to lose. And for the second week in a row they lost a critical game. The winning coach on the other hand ... sat impassively in the stands. The sign he gave to his players with this emotionless posture was that if the players wanted to win, they had to do it themselves. And they did. Just."

Both these coaches were very experienced and knowledgeable about the game. Both had got their teams to the finals. But why did

INTRODUCTION | ARE YOU POSITIVE OR NEGATIVE?

one coach's team always lose the close games and the other team always win?

It depends on the positive or negative outlook we project which can dramatically impact those around us. Often we are not aware of the messages we are sending through our language and actions. Psychologists call this a Locus of Control (first developed by Julian Rotter, 1966).

Locus of Control refers to a person's perception of the main causes of the events in their life. For example do you believe that your destiny is controlled by you – "I did it myself" – or by external forces such as fate or other people – "It was their fault", or "It was just a lucky break"? Put simply, if you believe that your behaviour is guided by your personal decisions and efforts then you are said to be more internally focused, that is you have an internal locus of control. On the other hand, if you believe that your behaviour is guided by fate, luck or other external circumstances, then you are said to have an external locus of control.

Is one better than the other? Psychologically, that's the $64,000 question. Generally people with an internal locus of control tend to have greater influence on their motivation, expectations, self-esteem, risk-taking behaviour and even on the actual outcome of their actions. As you would expect some studies also suggest that people with an internal locus of control tend to be more positive in their behaviour and outlook.

Do you know what your locus of control is? Perhaps the people who know you well are better placed to answer this for you. But there are also a number of short tests freely available on the web that only take a few minutes to complete and give you a good guide to your locus.

A second and probably more important question is: If you decide that you need to be more internally focused, can you change your locus of control?

INTRODUCTION | ARE YOU POSITIVE OR NEGATIVE?

The answer is an unequivocal "Yes".

Many studies show that our locus of control is something we have learned and therefore can be changed. My own experience in working as a coach to club, national and international rowing coaches is that training coaches by getting them to change their behaviour with their athletes improves the positive outlook the coaches display within 12 months. This approach has also been successful in my role as a training consultant in the work environment with new and aspiring managers who were looking to improve the motivation of their teams.

How do you change your own locus of control and consequently your outlook? There are a number of training programs available that use effective behavioural change methods to help move people from an external focus to an internal focus. But if you want a very simple method that you can start applying straight away, then changing the words you use in every day conversations can have a major impact.

For instance getting rid of the word 'don't' from your vocabulary and replacing it with the positive image of what you are suggesting begins to make you far more positive in your outlook. Take a look at the following short statements and see what images you get when you read each one (read the statement and see in your mind's eye what it is suggesting) ...

- *Don't drop it.*
- *Don't walk on the grass.*
- *In case of fire do not use lifts (or elevators).*

In the first statement the image that comes to mind is the picture of 'dropping something' and quite often the negative consequences of doing so. This reminds us of our previous negative experiences of dropping something, particularly when we were children.

INTRODUCTION | ARE YOU POSITIVE OR NEGATIVE?

The image that the second statement conjures up is of a person walking on the grass, not the footpath as the message intends. Note that 'footpath' is not mentioned.

And in the third example, the only thing we visualise is the lift. In fact studies show that when there is a fire emergency and the vestibule or foyer starts to fill with smoke, the only word that people recognise in these warning signs is the word 'lift' – they immediately head straight for the lift, not the emergency exit as was intended. As a result some authorities have now changed their signage to read 'In case of fire, use the emergency exit pictured in this diagram' (notice that in this new example the word 'lift' is not used at all).

Start to get the picture? Each of the original statements immediately has both the sender and the receiver visualising and thinking of exactly the opposite (and negative) action that should be taken. However, by eliminating the word 'don't' and replacing it with the positive action you intend (as outlined below), you will start to think and behave more positively, impact your audience more positively and thus become more internally focused. Look at the way a person with an internal locus of control might express the three statements ...

- *Hold on to the glass very carefully.*
- *Walk on the footpath.*
- *In case of fire use the fire exit described in the diagram.*

In these new statements the receiver gets the positive, visual message immediately.

How this book is structured

My experience with the word 'don't' has been the inspiration for this book. In the first Chapter we'll explore the concept of eliminating

INTRODUCTION | **ARE YOU POSITIVE OR NEGATIVE?**

the word 'don't' from our vocabulary. In addition to a focus on 'don't', in the following Chapters I'll outline the evidence linking language and behaviour and how using appropriate language can impact your self-identity, self-esteem, public image, personal relationships, your career and much, much more.

This book is written for those of you who want to make some positive changes in your life. Some of the suggestions are quite simple, others are more demanding. I expect you'll pick and choose from those that best suit you.

The book is in three parts –
1. How words impact our behaviour,
2. Words to use, words to avoid and other influencing factors, and
3. Difficult conversations and how to manage these.

Part One: How words impact our behaviour

Each Chapter outlines a particular aspect of language and how it impacts behaviour, provides relevant research to support the theory and includes plenty of examples to make it easy to follow. Chapters conclude with a sprinkling of suggested activities or exercises to enable you to put theory into practice.

Part Two: Words to use, words to avoid and other influencing factors

This is a short but important section containing only three Chapters. In the first two we look at common everyday words which often confuse people and at worst may cause conflict and emotional upset. The third Chapter describes a process for managing conversations and introduces phrases that can be used in most conversations to make them more effective communication dialogues. This Chapter is an ideal lead in to Part Three.

INTRODUCTION | **ARE YOU POSITIVE OR NEGATIVE?**

Part Three: Difficult conversations and how to manage these

Chapters in this part are stand-alone, to be read as and when you need them. They cover conversations that may be – or may become – difficult situations for either one or for both people. Examples include Parenting – how to converse with teenagers on difficult topics, Teenagers – how to converse effectively with parents, Friends – how to give a difficult message, Asserting – how to be more assertive when necessary, and many more situations which can be challenging for us. In many I've included some practice exercises and suggest strategies to employ in your next 'difficult' conversation – others do not require practice, just some guidance.

Are there more than words to communication?

While this book focuses on the words we use and how they impact on our own and others' behaviour, it's true that there's more to communication than the words. All face-to-face communication includes tone of voice, gestures, facial expressions and so on. Even in written communication, it's important to understand how the reader might interpret the sender's written message when the recipient uses the 'voice in their head' to read the words. For example, read the following sentence and note your first impression of its intent:

"I did not say she stole the money"

Now see if you can find the other five meanings (yes, there are at least six different ways of interpreting this simple sentence).

Communication therefore has many elements. In this book I'm focusing on the words and the tone of voice – I'll leave it to other writers to expand on the further very important facets.

INTRODUCTION | ARE YOU POSITIVE OR NEGATIVE?

Some readers may at first be sceptical about how simple words can change the way we think and act. I used to feel a bit like that too. For the present, can I ask you to be a little open minded until you can examine the evidence?

I read some time ago that in Eastern philosophy, Zen masters strive to have an empty cup:

> *"An empty cup has plenty of room to accept a fresh pour of tea, but a cup that is already full has no room left for anything new."*

Is your cup empty and ready for that fresh pour of tea?

Finally, if there's only one change you try from this book, please make it the 'don't' exercise in Chapter One. I'm convinced that if this concept were taught in our schools and people used it every day, the world would be a far more positive place – we'd all be thinking, talking and behaving about how things should and can be done rather than the roadblocks that are stopping us.

PART ONE
How words impact our behaviour

Introduction to Part 1

Part 1 outlines the building blocks for developing a positive outlook through using more positive language. It describes five mechanisms that you can apply to develop this positive outlook in everything that you do.

Chapter 1: *"Impact of the word 'don't' – Can you actually influence the behaviour of others?"* will show how simply eliminating the word 'don't' from your vocabulary can help you develop some great influencing skills.

Chapter 2: *"Choose the best words, become more positive – Can certain words we regularly use affect our own behaviour?"* This Chapter continues the positivity theme by introducing the skill of 'priming'. Some fascinating recent research demonstrates how easy it is to change our behaviour by choosing certain words – and you can do this easily and quickly in any situation.

Chapter 3: *"What impact does our 'personal' language have on our behaviour? – Can words affect how much you save? How much you eat? How

PART ONE | HOW WORDS IMPACT OUR BEHAVIOUR

much safe sex you have?" I hope this title has you salivating already! According to certain research, our mother tongue has a major impact on our behaviour. So some people have an unfair advantage (it's called the 'Futureless Concept') when it comes to matters such as saving habits. This Chapter will show how you can benefit from this research no matter what your first language is.

Chapter 4: "Metaphors and the use of 'and' – How clean is our language?" This Chapter introduces the concept of 'Clean Language' and builds on the powerful visual influence metaphors have in understanding one another when in conversation. I'll also suggest using 'and' to uncover the true meaning or feeling behind what someone else is expressing when they use a metaphor, particularly in a stressful situation.

Chapter 5: "How to use words, metaphors and actions to affect your feelings – Can what we say influence how we feel?" Here the metaphor theme continues plus I'll show how changing the words you use (either to yourself or others) can change how you feel. This can be particularly useful when you're feeling a little low or you need some self-motivation.

The first five Chapters have a range of suggestions and exercises you can use to apply the techniques that I trust will be very useful for you. Pick and choose the ones that best suit you and your situation.

Chapter 6: "How positive and negative words affect brain power – Can the words we use change the way our brain functions?" This final Chapter in Part 1 summarises some of the amazing research that shows what happens to our brains when we use certain words. I trust it provides you with a compelling argument to try out some of the techniques covered in the previous five Chapters.

CHAPTER 1

Impact of the word 'don't'

Can you actually influence the behaviour of others?

I remember standing in a gift store in Canberra, Australia some years ago when a mother with two young boys entered the shop. At their age of about three or four the only thing children want to do is to touch and feel things – to explore. The store was stacked full of open shelves with many delicate and breakable items such as glass and chinaware. If you were the boys' parent, what would be your natural instruction to your children?

In those days my instructions would probably have been "Don't touch anything". I'm pretty sure your instructions might have been quite similar.

By using an instruction such as "Don't touch anything" the only *visual image* the boys receive is 'touch anything'. Although we put the word 'don't' in front of 'touch anything', there is absolutely no visual image for the word 'don't'. The boys are left with the image of the act of touching anything (and knowing boys of that age, probably touching everything).

Not only is there no image for 'don't', it creates a further problem. People, and particularly children, have to double-process. The child has to think "What does she NOT want me to do?" as well as "What does she want me TO DO instead?" This can be very confusing, especially for young children as they may not know or understand the 'to do' part or have difficulty accessing it in memory.

Those of you who are parents will probably remember the many necessary corrective actions or commands which have to follow the instruction of "Don't touch anything" (it rarely works).

You could surmise that this is simply 'children being children', or 'boys will be boys'. I believe there's another reason.

Let's return to the mother and her boys. Instead of saying "Don't touch anything" to my surprise she actually said "Boys, keep your hands in your pockets until we get back outside this shop". Here the image is of 'putting hands in pockets' – there is no mention of touching anything. Not only has she given them a positive instruction of what to do, she's also put a finish-time on it: "until we get back outside this shop". Brilliant! That experience has stayed with me for many years.

The impact of giving positive instructions with an image of what you want the child to do rather than putting 'don't' in front of what you want them not to do can be seen immediately. If you're a parent, try it out sometime.

Similar results can also be obtained quickly with adults. For instance as an instructor to rowing coaches at the Academy of Sport in Sydney, I was able to introduce a new form of visual instruction into the coaches' repertoire. For example, a smooth action in rowing is essential to ensure the rowing skiff remains balanced and moves forward at the fastest possible speed. One thing that can prevent full effectiveness is if rowers move up the slide (moving seat) too quickly. So the coach would normally say "Don't move up the slide so quickly". By now you can see the point. The only image the rower received from this instruction was "move up the slide quickly" so they often did.

CHAPTER ONE | IMPACT OF THE WORD 'DON'T'

Once the coaches learned the 'don't' rule, i.e. *'Completely eliminate the word 'don't' from your vocabulary'*, their instructions changed to "Move up the slide slowly and smoothly". The resulting improvement in technique was immediate as the rowers were now receiving a very positive description of what the coach wanted them to do.

It was interesting to see the long-term results on rowers when their coaches eliminated 'don't' from their vocabulary. When interviewing the athletes some twelve months after the coaches had changed their method of instruction, the athletes universally commented on how much more positive their coaches had become, e.g., "I'm not sure what you did or what training you put her through, but she is so much more positive now". The athletes had not been told about the 'don't' rule, but had obviously been impacted by its results. And simply eliminating 'don't' also had an influence on the coaches' demeanour and attitude, quite possibly influencing their relationship with their rowers.

In addition to 'don't' being quite ineffective when given as an instruction, it can also be quite dangerous and even costly, as an Australian Government department found out just recently. Australia's tax collection agency has been involved in a lengthy compensation battle after a staff member's desk and chair heights were changed without her knowing.

The ergonomic stuff-up happened even though she had a sign on her work station reading 'do not adjust or sit at this desk'.

According to the press report, the initial compensation offered and the ensuing 18-month legal tussle demonstrated the potential liabilities of hot-desking where multiple workers use the same work station at different times. However, we know the real cause of the problem – her sign read 'do not <u>adjust or sit at this desk</u>'. How would you have worded the sign if you wanted people to stay clear of your desk?

Don't — *How using the right words will change your life*

As well as the majority of us, regulatory authorities also fall into the 'don't' trap. I mentioned earlier in the introduction to this book the examples of:

- *Don't walk on the grass.*
- *In case of fire do not use lifts (or elevators).*

Here are some signs I've seen that also fall into the 'don't' trap:

	Be honest with this one – who of us has not touched a seat or fence or wall when we've seen this sign, just to check whether it's still wet? Prior to understanding about 'don't', my belief is that we probably thought it was merely human nature to ignore the sign – whereas in fact we were not ignoring the sign, but following what it was inadvertently telling us to do – touch! **If you had to put up a 'Wet Paint' sign, what would it say?**
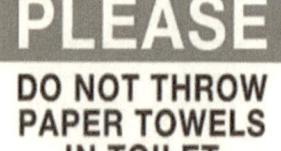	Note in this example the authorities try to improve on 'don't' by changing it to 'DO NOT' (they're also being polite by adding 'Please' in very large print). Does it make any difference? Unlikely! The only image we still get is to '(Please) throw the paper towels in the toilet'. **How would you re-word this with a positive message and image?**

CHAPTER ONE | IMPACT OF THE WORD 'DON'T'

DON'T EVEN THINK ABOUT PARKING HERE	*This one has really got me going – they've not only broken the 'don't' rule, they've also asked us to start thinking about the image of parking here (I'm already looking around to see whether my car will fit in this space).* *How would you re-word this with a positive message?*
SAFETY NOTICE In the unlikely event of an emergency please **DO NOT PANIC** and follow the crew's instructions	*I love this sign, it's one of my favourites (seen on a ferry boat in Ireland).* *What's the message in this sign? The words in upper case, bold and red, read 'DO NOT PANIC' – I'm already starting to feel a bit queasy just reading it now. What's their intention?* *How would you re-word this with a positive image?*

Below is an example of how a sign can be made positive very simply (and without words). On the left is the negative example 'Don't Walk' (the image given by the words? – 'Walk'). On the right is the better way to do it – walk is not mentioned – in fact we have the image of a hand raised in the traditional 'stop' pose (so we automatically visualise ourselves stopping):

Don't — *How using the right words will change your life*

PART ONE | **HOW WORDS IMPACT OUR BEHAVIOUR**

Here's another very positive sign …

This positive sign has caused us to pause, 'Think', and then given us the positive instruction 'Bend knees when lifting'. There's also an image of the person obeying the instruction.

I've also recently seen and heard some good news on eliminating 'don't' amongst professional football referees and umpires (of various codes). In past times when a player was called out for an infringement, say fighting, the conversation may have gone:

Referee: *"I don't want to see that behaviour again"*
Player: *"But he started it. I only retaliated after he hit me"*
Referee: *"I saw what happened. I don't want to hear any more"*

You'll readily recognise the referee's use of 'don't' where he is reinforcing 'that behaviour' and 'hearing more'. Although the

CHAPTER ONE | IMPACT OF THE WORD 'DON'T'

referee is trying to have the last word and get play started again, you can bet that the player will have more to say (and often quite heatedly). If this continues both the player and the referee are likely to become emotionally involved in the conversation. So now the heated conversation between referee and player becomes the focus and needs to be quelled – no doubt you've also witnessed similar heated exchanges between players and referees.

Referees that have learnt to eliminate 'don't' from their language now approach the situation quite differently. Firstly, it is likely that both players will be called out:

> Referee: *"I need to deal with this situation. I will talk with B first* (the victim) *then with you* (player A the perpetrator)*"*
> Referee turning to A: *"Walk away. I'll be with you shortly"*
> Player A: *"But he started it. I only retaliated after he hit me"*
> Referee: *"Walk away (or 'step away'). I'll hear your explanation shortly. Now step away"*

Notice in this scenario the referee has:
- Clearly outlined what will happen and how the situation will be managed
- Given a definite instruction to the player – "Walk away", "Step away"
- Stamped his authority on the situation through the positive language used

By now I trust that the picture is becoming clear. Yes, words can certainly impact the behaviour of others – and we can wield a great deal of influence by getting the words right.

So whether you're a parent, teacher, manager, salesperson or simply someone interested in becoming more positive and thus improving your ability to influence, the message is:

PART ONE | **HOW WORDS IMPACT OUR BEHAVIOUR**

Completely eliminate the word 'don't' from your vocabulary

Sounds easy? Perhaps. But from my own experience it does take a fair bit of discipline and practice – in fact it probably took me about twelve months to become really good at it.

If you'd like to start down the path of becoming more positive and improving your ability to influence others, try the following short exercise. Re-write the following signs/statements; eliminate the word 'don't' and use the positive words to emphasise the behaviour you want from people:

An inappropriate 'don't' statement:	An appropriate positive statement is:
• Don't drop it	
• Don't walk on the grass	
• In case of fire do not use lifts (or elevators)	
• Wet Paint. Don't Touch	
• Please do not throw paper towels in toilet	
• Don't even think about parking here	
• In the unlikely event of an emergency, please don't panic and follow the crew's instructions	
• Don't run across the road	

CHAPTER ONE | **IMPACT OF THE WORD 'DON'T'**

An inappropriate 'don't' statement:	An appropriate positive statement is:
• Don't tear that up	
• Don't lean on doors (sign seen on sliding doors in a commuter train)	
• Don't make jokes about bomb threats or terrorists (sign at the check-in counter at Sydney international airport)	
• Configuring updates – don't turn off your computer	
• Do not discard	
• Don't stand on moving footway (sign seen on a very narrow moving footway a.k.a. moving walkway or travelator)	
• Don't hold back	
• Don't go near the edge	

The Next Steps to eliminate 'don't' from your vocabulary ...

The previous exercise should have been easy. If you need to check your responses or perhaps see a different response, you can see my suggestions at the back of the book.

Exercise 1: How to practise eliminating 'don't' with a friend

Now it's a matter of changing your day-to-day language. It will help if you can work with a partner, friend or colleague – their role is to let you know when you've expressed something very positively (they could give you a visual sign such as a 'thumbs up'), or to pick you up when you inadvertently slip-up and use the 'don't' word. To avoid embarrassment or an interruption to the flow of the conversation, it may be best if they let you know after the situation has ended or the conversation has finished.

Exercise 2: How to change your regular 'don't' statements into positive instructions

Think about some of the instructions you are most likely to give on a day-to-day basis. For example if you're a parent there will probably be a lot of 'Don't do ...' statements. Write four or five of these out below and then prepare for your day by writing out the alternative, positive statement:

'don't' statements I often use:	I'll rewrite – and eliminate the word 'don't' as:

Review your results at the end of the day and repeat the exercise tomorrow (one of my friends recorded some of her conversations with her children and also a meeting at work, then played them back a number of times to check on her 'Don't' progress).

Exercise 3: How to make sure your changes are on track

Make a note in your diary to review your progress on these first two exercises at the end of the week. If you're working with a partner, also ask for some more feedback. In particular, bring to mind those times that you accidentally used 'don't'. Re-word your statements in the positive.

You may like to repeat these two exercises and gradually improve your effectiveness.

Exercise 4: How to break the 'don't' habit with a 21-day plan

Start your own 21-Day practice session by setting yourself the target of not saying 'don't' for the next 21 days.

Make a note in your diary to review your progress on a particular day of each week at a designated time. For example, "I am checking progress on my 21-day plan on Mondays at 9am". Please note the way this statement is expressed – in the present tense ("I am checking") as if it's already happening. We'll be discussing why expressing 'to do' statements such as this in the present tense is so important in a future Chapter.

PART ONE | **HOW WORDS IMPACT OUR BEHAVIOUR**

Exercise 5: How to work with your family, friends or colleagues at work to eliminate 'don't'

This can be a fun exercise – although it does require you to do some convincing of others to participate. Maybe you could give them a copy of this Chapter as a starting point so that they understand the concept.

Suggestions:

1. Identify any 'don't' signs around your home or work-place and have them changed into the positive (I encountered one recently at my physiotherapist that read 'Don't leave trolleys in this passage way'. After explaining the 'don't' rule to them, they changed it to 'Keep this passageway clear at all times' (notice in the new sign that trolleys are not mentioned).
2. Give this Chapter of the book to your family, friends or team and have a joint discussion on the topic of "Eliminating 'don't' from our place". Consider making this a bit of fun by having rewards for those who go a day/week etc. without saying 'don't' and a small penalty (such as a gold coin donation to charity) every time someone slips up and uses 'don't'.
3. Review progress at the end of each week.

A final comment:

I'm really interested to hear the results of your changes: Also if you happen to come across any unusual or funny 'don't' signs, please send them to me (www.therightwords.co). And do please keep in mind examples such as the wet paint sign which was actually telling us to 'touch the paint' – there is a much more positive way to influence others.

CHAPTER 2

Choose the best words – become more positive

Can certain words we regularly use affect our own behaviour?

So far we've seen how using certain words and phrases and eliminating the word 'don't' can be useful in helping us to directly influence the behaviour of others. It can also vicariously (over time) help us to become more positive in our outlook. But is there a more direct way we can influence what we do through what we say? Can the words we use have an immediate impact on us?

Let's look at some of the research.

For example, using hand held phones and electronic devices while driving is now banned in many countries. The evidence that using such devices while driving can lead to more accidents is overwhelming.

There's also a growing body of research which suggests even using hands-free mobile devices while driving increases the risk of accidents as much as using hand-held devices.

So if listening (and speaking) while driving and using electronic devices is considered dangerous, what about the actual words that are being used? For instance do certain words we use have greater impact on our driving behaviour than others?

To answer this question, in 2007 researchers at the Universities of Neuchatel, Zurich and Heidelberg (Prof. Marianne Schmid Mast) tested 83 male students between the ages of 20 and 27 in a high-end driving simulator. As they 'drove' music and words were played as if they were listening to the car radio. Unbeknown to the subjects, the researchers were testing to see if certain words had any impact on their driving behaviour.

Astonishing results: When the young male drivers heard masculine-sounding words such as 'muscle' or 'beard', they speeded up (and the speed remained faster till the end of the driving session). Conversely, when they heard feminine-sounding words such as 'pink' and 'lipstick' they slowed down. There were no speed differences when the male subjects heard neutral words. These results were statistically significant. This study provides compelling evidence of the impact certain words have on our behaviour.

But wait, there's more …

In 1996, researchers John Bargh, Peter Gollwitzer and their colleagues had subjects play a resource dilemma game. The game involved subjects competing against others in a simulated fishing contest from a community pond with the aim of catching as many fish as possible, maximising profits (they were paid for the fish they caught) and winning the game. The challenge however, was that players could only take out so many fish before the pond became depleted; each player then had to decide whether to take a fish or put it back for the betterment of the community.

Unbeknown to the subjects they were primed in a number of different ways (Barch, Gollwitzer and colleagues actually carried out many variations of this experiment, as they were also interested in the effects of goal setting on behaviour – however, here we look at just three of their variations). Prior to the experiment the first group was given a series of random words from which they had to construct

CHAPTER TWO | CHOOSE THE BEST WORDS – BECOME MORE POSITIVE

sentences. A second group was given a series of scrambled words that all stressed cooperation such as 'helpful', 'support', 'cooperative', 'fair' and 'share' from which they had to construct sentences. A third group was given no pre-reading nor sentence construction but were given explicit instructions that they must cooperate in the game if they were to be successful.

Bargh and Gollwitzer discovered that the simple act of reading and constructing sentences with cooperative words beforehand had a remarkably powerful effect on the subsequent behaviour of the participants. Specifically, the participants who used synonyms for 'cooperative' in their priming sentences returned 25 per cent more fish to the community pond than the people who were not exposed to these words.

Perhaps even more impressive was the fact that these cooperation-primed participants returned the exact same number of fish on average as participants who were explicitly primed in their instructions to act cooperatively.

So the evidence is really mounting that the words we use not only influence others, but can actually influence our own behaviour.

What does that mean for us?

Does it mean that we have to be more careful with the words we use? Perhaps. Think about the discussion in the Introduction about Locus of Control. If you want to become more internally focussed and take more responsibility for your own development, one way of doing this is to start using positive words and sentences.

However, as a starting point this requires some form of self-evaluation, which in essence is hard to do. How do you know or how can you tell that you are using more negative words than positive words or vice versa?

One way would be to ask someone else for their opinion. However, this could be quite tedious and may be a little intimidating (for both of you).

There's a suggestion on how to do this effectively at the end of this Chapter. In the meantime it would be useful to become aware of some of the more common negative and positive words so that you can make decisions about which to avoid and which to use.

For some time, people in certain occupations have been aware of the positive and negative impact of words when interacting with others. For instance in the sales profession and amongst skilled negotiators, it's long been known that some sentences are written to convey an affirmative or negative connotation in order to influence or persuade a reader. Specific words are chosen to construct this affirmative or negative tone. The words purposely chosen to express a negative idea are sometimes referred to as a 'negation'. The following lists are common negative words, adverbs and verbs used to illustrate a negative idea.

Negative words:	Negative Adverbs:	Negative verbs:
• No	• Hardly	• Doesn't
• Not	• Scarcely	• Isn't
• None	• Barely	• Wasn't
• No one		• Shouldn't
• Nobody		• Wouldn't
• Nothing		• Couldn't
• Neither		• Won't
• Nowhere		• Can't
• Never		• Don't (my favourite!)

CHAPTER TWO | CHOOSE THE BEST WORDS – BECOME MORE POSITIVE

Have a quick look back through these lists. Do you see any that you use regularly? I'm not suggesting that these words should never be used (just used one myself – 'never'). However, the overuse or regular use of a number of these negations not only influences our behaviour (as has been shown in the research) but can actually influence the way in which we perceive the world – in a positive or negative way.

Mark Waldman and Andrew Newberg in *Words Can Change Your Brain*, report that in addition to causing a negative perception of how we see the world, negative words have a damaging effect on our brain. For example flashing the word 'NO' on a screen for less than one second produces a sudden release of dozens of stress-producing hormones and neurotransmitters in the people watching the screen. These chemicals immediately interrupt the normal functioning of our brain, impairing logic, reason, language processing, and communication. However, (and unfortunately) using positive words (for example flashing the word 'YES' on a screen) does not have the opposite and immediate positive affect on our brain. In fact studies have shown that because negative words are so harmful to the brain, we need to produce a minimum of five positive words to counterbalance the harmful impact of one negative word.

All this suggests that we need to work harder at producing positive words both in our conversations and in our self-talk.

Unfortunately, as well as common negative words we may use from time to time, there are also a number of negative phrases that many of us use on a regular basis. These are particularly evident when we are attempting to do some difficult or new task and we use that 'voice in our head' to try and give us a little momentum or motivation to get going.

Some common ones that I have used in the past and I often hear others using aloud (and that I'm now eliminating) are "That's not a bad idea", "No problems" and the quintessentially Australian "No

PART ONE | HOW WORDS IMPACT OUR BEHAVIOUR

worries mate". All of these are intended as positive ideas or suggestions whereas they are reinforcing the negative – 'bad idea', 'problems' and 'worries'.

Here are 21 common self-talk phrases. Can you recall yourself using any of these? What do you say – either to yourself or aloud – when you are faced with a decision about which you're not sure, or a conundrum or perhaps a perplexing challenge?

At the end of this Chapter I've included this list again as an exercise to practise turning these negative self-talk phrases into positive. In the meantime, try to pick out the ones (or similar ones) that you use more frequently.

1. What if I try and fail?
2. This is difficult … (or, this is really difficult)
3. I can't do that …
4. If only I were … I would …
5. Why does this always happen to me? (or, not happen to me?)
6. I never get anything right …
7. I'm stuck in this rut …
8. I'm such a screw-up
9. I wish I had …
10. There goes another opportunity …

CHAPTER TWO | CHOOSE THE BEST WORDS – BECOME MORE POSITIVE

11.	I'll never get there
12.	I seem to be cursed
13.	Why doesn't this work for me?
14.	He'll / She'll never change
15.	My kids don't respect me
16.	I can't lose weight
17.	My boss ignores me
18.	Why don't I ever get a break?
19.	I have no time to exercise
20.	I'll never get out of debt
21.	He / She never listens

Find any that you use?

I trust by now that it's becoming evident that we need to be more mindful of the words we use to ensure we are being positive, or to become a more positive person. In my own case, I got rid of the word 'don't' about 15 years ago. Since then I've had many people tell me that "You always seem so positive about things – you've always got a good suggestion or recommendation to make" (actually they probably made the suggestion, I just prompted). For me, that's great feedback for an author, trainer and management consultant.

Perhaps you've had some similar feedback. If not, following is a short exercise to get you started down that positive track (I've completed the first two as examples).

Here's the negative 'self-talk' phrase	Turn these into positive 'self-talk' phrases
1. What if I try and fail?	1. This will work for me
2. This is difficult …	2. Challenges are there to be overcome
3. I can't do that …	3.
4. If only I were … I would	4.
5. Why does this always happen?	5.
6. I never get anything right …	6.
7. I'm stuck in this rut …	7.
8. I'm such a screw-up	8.
9. I wish I had …	9.
10. There goes another opportunity …	10.
11. I'll never get there …	11.
12. I seem to be cursed	12.
13. Why doesn't this happen for me? (or, Why does this always happen to me?)	13.

CHAPTER TWO | CHOOSE THE BEST WORDS – BECOME MORE POSITIVE

Here's the negative 'self-talk' phrase	Turn these into positive 'self-talk' phrases
14. He'll / She'll never change	14.
15. My kids don't respect me	15.
16. I can't lose weight	16.
17. My boss ignores me	17.
18. Why don't I ever get a break?	18.
19. I have no time to exercise	19.
20. I'll never get out of debt	20.
21. He / She never listens	21.

The Next Steps in choosing more positive words and phrases ...

That exercise should have been straightforward. If you need to check your responses or perhaps see a different response you can find my suggestions at the back of the book. Keep in mind the trick to embedding this positive approach in your personality is to regularly check your progress and adjust your words accordingly. The following activities are designed to do just that.

PART ONE | **HOW WORDS IMPACT OUR BEHAVIOUR**

Exercise 1: How to eliminate your negative self-phrases

Review the list of 21 negative self-phrases from the previous exercise. Which are the two or three (or perhaps you thought of another one) that you use regularly?
1. Write out the positive alternative 'self-phrase' on a small card, screen saver or somewhere where you will see it regularly.
2. Practise these new positive self-phrases daily.
3. Pick a particular day of the week for reviewing your progress. Record the date and time for review in your diary (Note: This step is particularly important for successful change).
4. Review your weekly progress and maintain the momentum for three weeks.

Exercise 2: How to turn your emails or texts into positive messages

Review the last five or six emails you have sent to someone asking for help, information or have made a specific request, OR where you have responded to a request for help or information:
- Find any negative statements/questions and reword them in the positive.
- If you now need something from someone, write them an email using positive statements.

Exercise 3: How to turn problem statements into solutions

Eliminate the word 'problem' from your vocabulary. When people hear 'problem' the automatic thinking is that something will be difficult, or can't be done, or that solutions have been unsuccessfully

CHAPTER TWO | CHOOSE THE BEST WORDS – BECOME MORE POSITIVE

tried before. Instead rephrase the issue as a 'challenge'. For example, "I think there's a problem with the timing for planting our bulbs – they do not flower at the right time. They're always late." could be rephrased as "I believe there's a challenge with getting the bulbs planted on time. What can be done to ensure they are planted in time so that they flower in Spring?" Notice that when using the word 'challenge' we automatically start to phrase things in the future tense, whereas problems are often described in the past tense (there'll be more on the use of tense in the next Chapter).

Exercise 4: How to prime yourself to be more positive

You'll recall how participants in the fishing contest mentioned earlier in this Chapter were primed to be cooperative. This is a simple and yet powerful technique that you can use regularly whenever you face a challenging conversation, difficult meeting or perhaps a tough negotiation.

Before your event, decide what you want to achieve. For example in a conversation with someone who is difficult you might decide "I'm being pleasant and agreeable throughout our talk" or if you have to face a difficult parent/teacher meeting (where you know your child has been at fault) you might decide "I'm listening (more than talking) throughout the discussion and gaining the teacher's respect and support".

When thinking about what you want to achieve, consider:
- What is it you want to happen during and following the event?
- How do you want to feel as a result?
- How do you want the other person to feel?

Answering these three questions will ensure you are well primed for your conversation, meeting or negotiation.

A final comment:

In our relationships negative language adds a barrier that need not be there. Sometimes negative language even causes conflict and confrontation where none is neither necessary nor desired.

The suggestions and exercises mentioned above will definitely put you on the right track towards using more positive language. My advice is that you start your change by using positive language in your written material – this will give you time to consider the best words to use. Once you have developed the knack of writing positively, it will be easier to change your spoken language to present a more positive tone.

And as that very old song goes …

You've got to accentuate the positive
Eliminate the negative
Latch on to the affirmative
Don't mess with Mister In-Between

Note: In addition to receiving feedback from others, you can test your positivity by undertaking the following tests:

- Mind Tools: Are You a Positive or Negative Thinker? at http://www.mindtools.com/pages/article/newTCS_89.htm
- 3 Smart Cubes: The Attitude Test at http://www.3smartcubes.com/pages/tests/attitudetest/attitudetest_instructions.asp
- Psychology Today at http://psychologytoday.tests.psychtests.com/

And there's a very good (and quick) self-test of your degree of optimism by Professor Elaine Fox, author of *Rainy Brain Sunny Brain: The New Science of Optimism and Pessimism* at http://www.rainybrainsunnybrain.com/bbc-horizon

CHAPTER 3

What impact does our 'personal' language have on our behaviour?

Can words affect how much you save? How much you eat? How much safe sex you have?

In Chapter 1 I discussed my experience with eliminating the word 'don't' and its impact on influencing others. In Chapter 2, we saw how certain words can influence our own behaviour. Let's go one step further and see how our mother tongue might also influence our behaviour.

M. Keith Chen, Associate Professor of Economics at UCLA, believes he's found an association between the language people use (i.e. their native tongue) and their ability to save for their retirement, to resist obesity, to stop smoking and indeed to practise safe sex.

Now if that's true, then this discovery is very powerful!

By the way they are structured, certain languages force us to express what we have done, are doing or plan to do, in the past, present or future tenses (the delineation is particularly evident between present and future). Such languages are often referred to by linguists as hard future tense languages (FTL) – and because of this people clearly separate present and future events, for example; "I am exercising" (present) and "I will exercise" (future). This tends to make the future seem far more distant to the speaker. English is one such hard FTL language, French is another.

Soft FTL languages such as Finnish, German, Dutch, Flemish and Chinese (both Mandarin and Cantonese) do not make such hard distinctions between today and the future. Here's an example of both hard and soft FTL:

In English (a hard FTL) speakers might say …

It *rained* yesterday   It *is raining* today   It *will rain* tomorrow

Whereas in German (a soft FTL) speakers on the other hand, might say …

Es regnete gestern   Es regnet heute   Es regnet morgen
(It *rained* yesterday)   (It *rains* today)   (It *rains* tomorrow)

As an economist, M. Keith Chen was originally investigating people's savings habits in comparison with the language they spoke.

CHAPTER THREE | WHAT IMPACT DOES OUR 'PERSONAL' LANGUAGE HAVE ON OUR BEHAVIOUR?

Chen's hypothesis is that because people speaking hard future languages (such as French and English – he called these 'futured' languages) have to viscerally separate the present from the future with the words they use, they find it harder to save money. That is every time they talk about the future, they disassociate the future from the present thus making it seem more different and more distant. For example in expressing a desire to save more, futured language speakers might say "I will start saving tomorrow".

Soft future language (which Chen calls 'futureless') speakers however, because they do not instinctively separate the present from the future in the words they use, would find it easier to save. It's just a seamless process to them, as they would say "I'm saving" (in both the present and future tenses).

For some time I've been acutely aware of the impact of language on the way we act. Until I read Chen's research, I was unaware of the 'present/future' dichotomy he describes. For instance, some years ago I developed a New Business Pack to help small businesses get started. In doing the research for the project, I found that one of the major reasons for failure amongst small businesses is the lack of planning. In addition to the lack of formal planning this included the lack of taking a future oriented approach. Although many small business operators see the need for planning, they just tend to avoid it – and if they do make a plan, they often fail to follow it. So in the New Business Pack we studiously avoided using the words 'plan' or 'planning'. It may have been that I was unconsciously taking a 'soft future' approach. If developing the pack today, I think I'd now be far more conscious of the need to seamlessly mix the present with the future.

In Chen's studies, he found that futureless language speakers save up to 30% more per annum than their futured language counterparts. The figure for retirement savings was 25% higher for futureless speakers. This difference held true even in countries where there was more than one language spoken in different parts of the country (e.g. French and Flemish in Belgium, French and German in Switzerland).

This result was quite amazing. Even more surprising, not only were there differences in savings habits, there were also differences in health habits – for example futureless speakers were:
- 20-24% less likely to smoke
- 13-17% less likely to be obese
- 21% more likely to use condoms

If you are a native futured language speaker (as I am) you may now be starting to get a bit worried about your retirement and perhaps your health. If not worried, then maybe a little envious of others who have a natural advantage due to the language they speak. Hang in there – good news is coming.

Chen and his colleagues are currently working on how futured language speakers may improve their ability to save and increase their healthy life experiences. That work is yet to be published. In the meantime, and in keeping with the ideas already set out in in this book, here are some of my suggestions.

Remember, the Futureless Concept is:

> *"Express the future action as if it is already happening."*

What to do next

Start rephrasing the way you describe the future as being similar to the present, for example:
- "It will rain tomorrow" could be expressed as "It rains tomorrow?" (Spoken with an upward inflection and with a

CHAPTER THREE | WHAT IMPACT DOES OUR 'PERSONAL' LANGUAGE HAVE ON OUR BEHAVIOUR?

question mark). This one may be a little hard to get used to. However, persevere. Those of you in an English-speaking country may now see why new arrivals from futureless speaking countries learning English, often say "It rains tomorrow" rather than the grammatically correct "It will rain tomorrow". For example my wife whose first language is Dutch says "What <u>*are we doing*</u> for the holidays", whereas I say "What <u>*are we going to do*</u> for the holidays?" (That's probably why she is always talking about activities months before I get around to thinking about them – but I'm starting to learn the futureless technique!).

- "I will start saving tomorrow" now becomes "I am saving".
- "I will stop smoking" now becomes "I walk for 5 minutes every time I feel like smoking" (in keeping with our 'don't' rule, notice that although the word 'smoking' is used, it's preceded by the action of 'walking' and has a time boundary attached, making it a positive image of 'walking for 5 minutes').

In all of the above examples, the action is expressed as if it is already happening, i.e.

- *Raining*
- *Saving*
- *Walking*

So remember, the guideline here (for us futured speakers) is to **express the future action as if it is already happening.**

The Next Steps in merging the Present with the Future

Exercise 1: How to learn the futureless concept using your New Year's resolutions

Here's a practical way to start thinking about implementing this Futureless Concept:
- Jot down your New Year's resolutions from last year (or from whenever you made some)
- Now rewrite them as if they are already happening
- Express these to a friend or colleague (as if they are happening) and watch for their response

For example in my case I decided last year that I wanted to do more exercise by riding my bike more often. I expressed my New Year's resolution as "I really want to do more regular riding this year". Using the Futureless Concept, I would now express this as "I'm riding at least three times per week". Even though I may not have started this new regimen, it's spoken as if I have, thus making it a seamless transition from present to future (at the time of writing this Chapter, I've now ridden for 70 days straight, so the futureless concept is working for me).

Exercise 2: How to practise the futureless concept

Whenever you decide that you are going to do something new or different, and you really mean it:
- Write out the new behaviour as if it is already happening on a card, piece of paper, PC, tablet, phone etc. and place it where you will see it regularly (e.g. fridge or screen saver).

- Rather than start the item with "I'm going to …" or "I will …" start the item with "I am …" and phrase it in the present tense, not the future – thus assuming that it's already happening.

A final comment:

The Futureless Concept is quite easy to understand, yet a little more difficult to implement. After all if you are a natural futured language speaker, it's something you've done almost since birth, so it may be quite a tall order. However, if you persist by using some of the above techniques, it will start to make a difference in the way you approach problems, challenges and dare I say, the future.

PS. You can see M. Keith Chen's TED talk at: http://www.ted.com/talks/keith_chen_could_your_language_affect_your_ability_to_save_money?language=en#t-279198

CHAPTER 4

Metaphors and the use of 'and'

How clean is our language?

- That's music to my ears
- She ran like the wind
- I'm heartbroken
- It's raining cats and dogs
- He's bouncing off the walls
- A heated debate
- Chill out!
- Cool!
- You light up my life
- My memory is a little cloudy on that
- It's like beating a dead horse
- Let sleeping dogs lie
- Blind as a bat

Wink wink ... nudge nudge ... say no more ... do you recognise some of these sayings? Perhaps you've used one or more recently – as recently as in the last five minutes.

Yes, they are metaphors. And we use metaphors in every conversation we have. In fact some researchers suggest that we use about six metaphors every minute. They are a fabulous way of getting complicated messages across or merely speeding up the

CHAPTER FOUR | METAPHORS AND THE USE OF 'AND'

communication by saying in a few words what might otherwise take paragraphs. For example in discussing the untidiness of a teenager's bedroom, the parent could just say "it's a disaster area – it's like a bomb's hit it" and we'd all get the picture immediately, rather than having to describe the state of the room in detail.

The definition of a metaphor is "a figure of speech containing an implied comparison, in which a word or phrase ordinarily and primarily used of one thing is applied to another". For example, "the curtain of night" or "all the world's a stage."

Notice too that a metaphor is nearly always visual. For example, "a rollercoaster of emotions", "it stuck out like a sore thumb" or "it's raining cats and dogs". So not only does a metaphor shorten the communication process, it adds an image that triggers the visual part of the brain and enhances the prospect of the message being understood more clearly. Phrases such as metaphors that immediately access the visual part of the brain are particularly important for effective communication as most languages have words that have more than one meaning; for example in English it's been estimated as high as 80% of words have more than one meaning.

In *The Cambridge Handbook of Metaphor and Thought*, author Raymond W. Gibbs quotes some of the compelling scientific evidence that demonstrates the power of metaphors in communication, summarised here as:

- Metaphors are conceptual mappings; they are part of the conceptual system (of the brain) and not merely linguistic expressions.
- There is a huge system of fixed metaphorical mappings, which means these are universally understood.
- This system exists physically in our brains so that when we hear a metaphor it is easily accessed in the system.

- Because certain metaphors are grounded via previous correlated experiences, they make immediate sense, for example 'more' is up (grounded via the correlation between quantity and verticality – you pour more water in the glass and the level goes up).

In fact Gibbs makes a very important point: "Much of our reasoning makes use of conceptual metaphors."

So while it's easy to see how metaphors improve our communication processes, it's been found that they are even more important than that – we actually think metaphorically.

In 1980 two researchers George Lakoff and Martin Johnson published *Metaphors We Live By* which examined how, when and why we use metaphors. For example we understand *control* as being UP and *being subject to control* as being DOWN. We say, "I have control *over* him", "I am *on top of* the situation", "He's at the *height* of his power" and "He ranks *above* me in strength", "He is *under* my control" and "His power is on the *decline*". Similarly we describe love as being a physical force: "I could feel the *electricity* between us", "there were *sparks*" and "they *gravitated* to each other immediately".

But there may be even more to metaphors than we realise.

James Lawley and Penny Tomkins in *Metaphors in Mind* contend that the metaphors we use, while simplifying our communication can also hide deeper feelings and thoughts. They suggest that if the issue is really important to us what's behind these metaphors needs to be understood.

And in a physiological sense, a team of researchers from Emory University reported in *Brain & Language* that when subjects in their laboratory read a metaphor involving texture, the sensory cortex of the brain, responsible for perceiving texture through touch, became

CHAPTER FOUR | METAPHORS AND THE USE OF 'AND'

active. Metaphors such as "the singer had a velvet voice" and "he had leathery hands" roused the sensory cortex.

So it seems that science is telling us that using metaphors can have an impact on our thoughts, feelings and even senses!

And in terms of day-to-day communication with others, Lawley and Tomkins suggest a way that the listener can also better understand what the speaker actually means when using a metaphor by applying a technique called 'Clean Language' to clarify.

Clean Language is a questioning technique that was first used in psychotherapy and coaching. It has the client discover and develop personal symbols and metaphors without contamination or distortion through the way the questions are put. It is now being used far more widely in areas such as training, facilitation, marketing, negotiating, management and even IT.

Clean Language was first developed by David Grove (a New Zealander) in the 1980s as a result of his work on clinical methods for resolving clients' traumatic memories. As authors Lawley and Tompkins describe it, "He realised many clients naturally described their symptoms in metaphor, and found that when he enquired about these using their exact words, their perception of the trauma began to change."

Unlike other forms of communication, such as reflective listening where the listener reflects (and in so doing often interprets) what the other person might be feeling and thinking, Clean Language follows a series of questions that only use the other person's exact words to help them define their thoughts and feelings.

To ensure the questioner stays 'clean', every question starts with 'and'. This means that the questioner has to follow the 'and' with the person's exact words. It's how the questioner uses the other's exact words that gives Clean Language its power.

Here's an example of clean questioning used in a therapeutic context:

Client: *"It seems that I'm stuck with no way out."*

Clean Language Question: *"And **what kind of** stuck with no way out is that stuck with no way out?"* (Note: This phrasing may seem clumsy to the non-professional, but has been found by therapists to be most effective when phrased this way because it places emphasis on the client explaining what "stuck with no way out" is like and how it is affecting him/her.)

As Lawley and Tomkins suggest:

> *"This question works with the client's metaphor of stuck and only assumes that for something to be stuck it has to be stuck somewhere. When the therapist is in rapport with the metaphoric information, questions like the above make perfect sense, and client's responses have a quality of deep introspection and self-discovery. New awareness of their own process 'updates the system' and the original neural coding will automatically begin to transform; albeit in minute ways at first."*

Clean Language questions are then asked of the client of each subsequent response. The process ultimately accesses conflicts, paradoxes, double-binds and other 'holding patterns' which previously kept the symptoms repeating over and over rather than delve into the root cause.

In fact Lawley and Tomkins go so far as to suggest that "... whatever a person says, sees, hears, feels or does, as well as what they imagine, can be used to comprehend and reason through metaphor."

Now in a business context, one could also easily see how Clean Language (or an adaptation of it) could be readily used. For example, in a tense negotiation when the other person says "We seem to be stuck here with no way out", one could easily ask "and what kind of stuck

CHAPTER FOUR | METAPHORS AND THE USE OF 'AND'

is that stuck with no way out?" The resulting conversation might very well describe exactly the sticking point and most importantly, what it means to the other person.

All 'and' questions pick up on the metaphor the other person is using and find out what's really behind it, for example:
- "and that <u>bottleneck</u> is like what?"
- "and that <u>roadblock</u> is like what?"
- "and that <u>treading water</u> is like what?"
- "and that <u>impasse</u> is like what?"
- "and that <u>mind-set</u> is like what?"

So too in day-to-day conversations we can see how metaphors can improve the communication process. There should be one note of caution though: Metaphors can be culturally specific, so when purposely using a metaphor, choose your metaphor carefully when speaking with others from a different culture (I learnt this the hard way when speaking with my French daughter-in-law who speaks English fluently but had difficulty understanding the meaning of some of my Australian metaphors). There can also be cultural differences in the language used between English speaking countries, for example Australia and the US or the US and Great Britain.

To help you become familiar with metaphors here are some further examples:
- *Her lovely voice was* **music to his ears**
- *I need a new* **technique for my toolbox**
- *My kid's room looks* **like a bomb hit it**
- *We are being* **crushed by the weight** *of legislation*
- *You are* **my sunshine**
- *We must* **defend our market** *share*
- *We're going through a* **stormy phase**

- We have to **construct a new plan**
- I can't **digest all these facts**
- We were **sprouting new ideas** all over the place
- The management has **to move on** if they don't want **to be left behind**
- Our values are at the **heart of this organisation**
- We have **given birth** to a new generation of products
- We've **buried our head in the sand** about the competition

And here's a great example from an executive who really understood how important metaphors can be when getting a message across. In terms of the importance of good communication in an organisation, he was asked; "Can you justify communication as a return on investment?" He responded: "Enormous! We can move faster, jump higher, dive deeper and come up drier than anybody else in the business. When we hang a left, everyone goes left. It gives us an enormous ability to work as a team. Other companies in our industry are yet to work that out."

Did you get a feeling of excitement and want to learn more about the communication process in his organisation? Hearing his colourful metaphorical explanation, I certainly did.

However, there can also be some limitations to the impact of metaphors if the metaphor has become dated or overused (where the meaning is understood, but the impact on a particular part of the brain is lessened). For instance, some scientists have contended that figures of speech such as 'a rough day' are so familiar that they are treated simply as words and no more, i.e. while still metaphors they've lost the impact they may have had originally. So using a metaphor such as 'at the end of the day' to describe an ultimate outcome, no longer conjures up in our brain the picture of a beautiful sunset topping off a wonderful day – they're just words.

CHAPTER FOUR | METAPHORS AND THE USE OF 'AND'

Yet there are also some very famous metaphors that stand the test of time and provide instant meaning, for example 'No man is an island'. Although originally from a poem by John Donne, 'No man is an island' has come to be used as a metaphor for 'the need for cooperation; for connection (with people and places)'. Here's part of Donne's original poem first published in 1624:

No Man is an Island

*No man is an island entire of itself; every man
is a piece of the continent, a part of the main;
if a clod be washed away by the sea, Europe
is the less, as well as if a promontory were, as
well as any manner of thy friends or of thine
own were; any man's death diminishes me,
because I am involved in mankind.
And therefore never send to know for whom
the bell tolls; it tolls for thee.*

Note also that this poem has spawned another very famous and well-used metaphor 'For whom the bell tolls'. It's truly astounding that these two metaphors from the one source have stood the test of time in their meaning and impact for almost 400 years: Yes both still access the sensing parts of the brain such as visual (island) and sound (bells) when heard today.

In summary, we all use metaphors every time we communicate, be it face-to-face or via some other means. Mostly we are not aware of using them as they seem to come from nowhere, but are there when we need them. The aim of this Chapter has been to raise your awareness of the importance of metaphors and how we can use them more knowingly to improve our communication intent and also our understanding of the meaning or feeling behind what others are saying.

The Next Steps for using Metaphors to improve your communication ...

Exercise 1: How to learn about metaphors by watching your favourite movie or TV show

When next watching your favourite movie or TV show, try to identify the metaphors and particularly the number of metaphors used in the first three minutes of dialogue. I think you'll be quite surprised by both the extent and the number. You might like to write down a couple that you remember – there's a very good likelihood that the remainder of the show or movie will bear out what was meant or felt by the characters when they first used the metaphor. This exercise will clearly demonstrate the powerful impact that metaphors have on communication and most importantly, the meaning behind what is being said.

Exercise 2: How to influence a difficult person by using metaphors

When next you are about to have a conversation with someone you've had difficulty getting your message across to in the past, do some brief preparation:
- What is it you want to communicate?
- How do you want the person to feel following the conversation?
- Now, write out at least five or six metaphors that you could use to achieve your aim.
- Beside each metaphor, complete the sentence "so that …". This will provide you with some very good examples of what you want the person to understand and how you would like them to feel at the end of the conversation.

CHAPTER FOUR | **METAPHORS AND THE USE OF 'AND'**

Exercise 3: How to practise using 'and' with a friend

When next you find yourself in a conversation with a friend who is trying to explain something new or difficult to you, place the word 'and' in front of the first metaphor they use and repeat it to them. Practise this as many times as you can with friends and colleagues (at the appropriate time and opportunity of course) so that it becomes quite natural for you.

Exercise 4: How to use 'and' in a difficult situation

Finally, once you feel comfortable using the 'and (metaphor)' technique, use it (appropriately) when next faced with a really difficult or confronting situation, to defuse the emotion or find out the reasoning or deep feeling behind what the other person is saying or implying. For example, when a good friend is sharing a difficult problem with you and they use a metaphor to describe their concern, you could add "and what type of (use their metaphor) is that (repeat their metaphor)?"

A final comment:

Metaphors, their impact and usage have been studied for many years now by various disciplines from linguists to neuro scientists. From all of the research it's clear that they play an important part in our communication.

In addition to being useful in many difficult conversations, in a future Chapter we'll be looking at how metaphors can also improve your presentations and public speaking.

And in terms of the Clean Language concept, since learning about it a few years back I've been using it very successfully in both personal and business situations. It certainly does give you a far greater depth of understanding of what others are saying and particularly how they are feeling, so I'd encourage you to give it a try.

CHAPTER 5

How to use words, metaphors and actions to affect your feelings

Can what we say influence how we feel?

Grin and bear it!

We've seen how words and phrases, and particularly metaphors, can impact our behaviour and thinking, but what about feelings? Can what we say also impact how we feel?

I was recently reading a LinkedIn posting by Tony Robbins in which he recounted a heated negotiation he and two partners had with another group. In conversation following the negotiation one of Robbins' partners was enraged and furious about how they had been treated, and said so. Robbins too was frustrated and angry, and said so. The other partner, while somewhat annoyed at the outcome, was relatively calm and merely described his feelings about their treatment as "being a little peeved". Robbins thought this was a bit weird and the word 'peeved' rather amusing. So much so that he started to think about how using a word such as 'peeved' might change one's feelings from say anger, to bemusement.

Over the next few weeks he decided to try this out.

PART ONE | **HOW WORDS IMPACT OUR BEHAVIOUR**

An opportunity soon arose when he checked into a hotel one evening after midnight. Robbins had a speaking engagement next morning at 8am. The late (or early morning) check-in was not going smoothly and he was becoming annoyed – he just wanted to sleep. Instead of expressing his annoyance and perhaps mounting anger, he merely mentioned to the desk clerk he was feeling a little "peeved". This immediately brought a smile to his face and that of the desk clerk. Robbins' annoyance subsided.

What's happening here?

The technical term is 'embodied cognition' (the idea that the mind is not only connected to the body but that the body influences the mind) initiated by priming – we can prime ourselves (and others) to think, feel and consequently behave differently by giving instructions to the brain either consciously or subconsciously by the words we use and/or the actions we take. We've already seen an example in Chapter 2 where subjects were primed to act cooperatively in a fishing game; now let's look at how priming can also affect our feelings.

Yale psychologist John Bargh is one of the foremost researchers in the area of embodied cognition. For instance one of his experiments showed that participants holding warm as opposed to cold cups of coffee were more likely to judge a confederate as more generous, caring and trustworthy after only a brief interaction (one question they were asked was how likely they would be to employ this person – those who had held the warm cups said "Yes" and those who held the cold cups said "No" or "Not sure").

How powerful is priming – the use of words, metaphors and actions to direct our thinking and feeling? Well, to illustrate here are some examples of experiments that he and others have carried out:

CHAPTER FIVE | HOW TO USE WORDS, METAPHORS AND ACTIONS TO AFFECT YOUR FEELINGS

- Thinking about the future causes people to lean slightly forward while thinking about the past causes people to lean slightly backwards. *Future is Ahead.*
- Squeezing a soft ball influenced people to perceive gender neutral faces as female while squeezing a hard ball influenced people to perceive gender neutral faces as male. *Female is Soft.*
- Those subjects who held heavier clipboards judged currencies to be more valuable and their leaders to be more important. *Important is Heavy.*
- Subjects asked to think about a moral transgression like adultery or cheating on a test were more likely to request an antiseptic cloth after the experiment than those who had thought about good deeds. *Morality is Purity.*
- Subjects who read a passage about an interaction between two people were more likely to characterise it as adversarial if they had first handled rough jigsaw puzzle pieces, compared to smooth ones. *Rough is Harsh.*
- Subjects sitting in hard, cushion-less chairs during a negotiation were less willing to compromise on price than people who sat in soft, comfortable chairs. *Hard is Tough.*

In all of these experiments (subjects were not told of their purpose) while the subjects' conscious focus was on a very specific task, their subconscious was deciding on how they should feel towards everything around them. Lawrence Williams, who helped design the warm coffee cup experiment with John Bargh says, "it's no coincidence that we use the same word — warmth — to describe both a physical and an emotional experience. Somewhere in the brain, those two sensations are linked."

Researchers such as Paul Eckman have found too that our old friend the metaphor is based on the physiology of emotions. For example 'happy' is up and 'sad' is down as in "I'm feeling up today" and "I'm feeling down in the dumps". It's no surprise then, that around the world people who are happy tend to smile and perk up while people who are sad tend to droop. Which do you do? (If you happen to be a sports fan, take notice of a team that is losing badly – their shoulders and heads droop – their bodies are indicating how badly they feel about the situation.)

How to use words to intensify or change your feelings

Using the suffix 'ing'

There's an interesting concept used in Neurolinguistics called 'Transderivational Morphology' which suggests that by adding prefixes or suffixes to words results in an internal sense of movement. So for example, adding 'ing' to nouns immediately increases our inner sense of movement as in 'hand → handing', 'flower → flowering', 'sleep → sleeping'. Joshua Cartright in his posting "The Word is… 'Unstucking': How changing your words can get your brain moving again…" suggests a simple way of doing this – try it for yourself – add 'ing' to each of the following and say each out loud:

- email → emailing
- rock → rocking
- smile → smiling

Notice how you get a real sense of movement when these are expressed as 'emailing', 'rocking' and 'smiling'. So adding 'ing' to some of the words we might use in general conversation when talking about

CHAPTER FIVE | HOW TO USE WORDS, METAPHORS AND ACTIONS TO AFFECT YOUR FEELINGS

our feelings can change how we feel. For example when you've had an interesting conversation with someone and you intend to take some positive action such as emailing them further information, instead of saying "I will email you about this" try saying "I'm emailing you about this".

Notice in this second statement "I'm emailing you about this" three things are transpiring:
- In your mind, the action of 'emailing' is already happening
- Your brain experiences a sense of movement
- Because this is expressed as if it's already happening (it's expressed in the present tense), you feel good about it.

You'll recall from Chapter 3 where phrasing statements about the future in the present tense as if they are already happening has a positive impact on our actions such as saving, health activities and so on. Now there's a further reason to use this technique – it also positively impacts how we feel.

I've also recently noticed a practical example of helping people feel good about themselves where a weight-loss specialist organisation – Jenny Craig – is using the 'ing' approach when marketing their programs. Their whole attention is directed at emphasising 'during' the program. Of course 'before and after' is highlighted, but the actual program is labelled 'During' – emphasising how people are feeling good about themselves as they proceed no matter how small the progress (they use the words "experience the during" in their ads).

Replacing 'but' with 'and'

And there's another very simple way of intensifying your feelings or making sure your positive feelings remain positive – that's reducing the use of 'but' in our sentences, particularly when talking about our feelings. In Chapter 7, I'll be discussing how the word 'but' can be a conversation buster. For the present let's look at how eliminating 'but' from our thoughts and statements can help us feel more positive. For instance, whenever we use 'but' in a sentence it tends to negate whatever has gone before or it puts a counter argument/proposal. For example a news report such as "The employment figures are good news, but only in the short term" is typical of negating the good news on employment with the use of 'but'. On a personal level you might say "I feel great, but it's raining" – immediately your 'great feeling' has been dissipated. A way to maintain that positive feeling is to replace 'but' with 'and' as in "I feel great and it's raining".

To test this, try saying each of these statements out loud:
- "I feel great, but it's raining"
- "I feel great and it's raining"

Feel the difference?

In Chapter 4 we saw how powerful the word 'and' can be in conversations with others; particularly in helping us understand how they are feeling. Now we have another use for 'and' – in conversations with ourselves and in statements we make to others to help us feel more positive about what we are doing, saying and ultimately feeling.

So returning to the question posed at the start of this Chapter; "Can what we say also impact how we feel?" it can be seen that the answer is a definite "Yes": It's been shown how words can impact our feelings. To paraphrase Tony Robbins, he was probably on the right track to "grin and bear it".

CHAPTER FIVE | **HOW TO USE WORDS, METAPHORS AND ACTIONS TO AFFECT YOUR FEELINGS**

Suggestions for using words and metaphors to change how you feel

Before concluding this Chapter and making some suggestions for applying these ideas, it's worth noting some of the research that may well impact your success. That is, if you want to change then it's not merely enough to think about doing something differently, it's vital that you 'objectify' it – you physically write it down.

To test this, researchers at the Universidad Autónoma de Madrid in Spain examined whether objectifying our thoughts can influence whether such thoughts are used in subsequent evaluations.

In the first experiment participants wrote about what they either liked or disliked (felt) about their bodies. They were then asked to either tear-up and throw away the paper on which they wrote their thoughts (feelings) or keep it and check for errors. When participants physically discarded a representation of their thoughts (by throwing the paper away) they mentally discarded their thoughts as well, using them less in forming subsequent judgments about their bodies than did participants who retained a representation of their thoughts. Those who retained their written thoughts and who wrote positive thoughts rated their bodies more favourably than before the test, and vice versa for those who wrote negative thoughts. But no change in body image was observed in people who threw away the paper.

A second experiment replicated this finding. It also revealed that these effects were stronger when the action was performed physically (by writing them down) rather than merely imagined.

A third experiment went one step further: It showed that people relied on their thoughts more when they not only wrote them down but also physically kept them in a safe place – i.e. they 'put their thoughts' (their feelings written on paper) in their pockets, wallets or purses – than when they discarded them.

These experiments are a further example of embodied cognition and show how important it is for us to actually take some action if we want to change things, particularly our feelings, rather than just thinking about them.

And now, some suggestions for using words and metaphors to change how you feel

Exercise 1: How to practise using words to change how you feel

1. Take a sheet of paper and draw vertical lines to divide it into three columns.
2. Think back over the last week. When can you remember feeling either very positive or very negative about something that happened? Try to think of three or four instances.
3. Keeping each of these instances in mind, write down the words that best express your feelings in each situation in the first column.
4. Once you have 10 or more feeling words, read back over them. In the second column, write 'positive' or 'negative' against each word. (My experience suggests you may have more negatives than positives).
5. In the third column against each of the negative words, write a new word that is a more positive or perhaps more humorous way of expressing this feeling. Think of Robbins' example of 'peeved' versus 'angry'. If you need help, go to the Thesaurus which can be a great guide (or you may care to replace the word with a metaphor, for example "I'm on top of this").

CHAPTER FIVE | **HOW TO USE WORDS, METAPHORS AND ACTIONS TO AFFECT YOUR FEELINGS**

6. In the coming week when you get into a situation where you start to feel somewhat negative, immediately use the new feeling word or metaphor you developed in a sentence or two. Notice how your negative emotions start to dissipate instead of intensifying. Go on to repeat this with some of your other negative feeling words as situations present themselves.

    Note: If you now look back over your positive words, you may also like to change them slightly to express an even more positive feeling, for example amplify 'happy' to 'delighted' or even 'blissful'.

Exercise 2: How to use the suffix 'ing' to enhance your positive feelings

If you undertook the exercise in Chapter 3 on the futureless concept, reflect on how you felt when you expressed your statements in the present tense. If you've not already completed that exercise, my suggestion is to try it now with one additional step.

Here's the exercise as it was described in Chapter 3 ...

Whenever you decide that you are going to do something new or different, and you really mean it:

- Write out the new behaviour as if it is already happening on a card, piece of paper, PC, tablet, phone etc. and place it where you will see it regularly (e.g. fridge or screen saver).
- Rather than start the item with "I'm going to ..." or "I will ..." start the item with "I am ..." and phrase it in the present tense, not the future – thus assuming that it's already happening.

The additional step is to:

- Read out the new behaviour aloud. Make sure it is expressed as if it's now happening and that the verb embodies the 'ing'

Don't — *How using the right words will change your life*

suffix as in "I am now exercising 15 minutes each morning before I go to work".

How are you feeling now about your proposed action?

You may also decide that it's worth trying this technique in general conversation. If so, keep an eye (and an ear) out for an opportunity to express an action or feeling as an 'ing' word (our earlier example of "I'm emailing you on this" is one that most people will use at some time, so you could try that one as a starter).

Exercise 3: How to change 'but' to 'and' to enhance your positive feelings

Whilst this technique sounds easy it's a little more difficult to do – after all, we've probably been using 'but' in our sentences for many years. One of the best ways I've found of changing this is to:

1. Decide on a conversation where you intend to try this technique. For example you might be meeting a friend for coffee (as I write this, I'm about to revisit my ability to use 'and' more than 'but' when I meet with a friend for coffee this morning).
2. Whenever you have a positive thought (or feeling) and you think there might be some small impediment to its success or implementation, try linking the two thoughts with 'and'.
3. After the conversation, reflect on many of your statements:
   - Where did you use 'and' successfully? How did you feel at the time?
   - Were there any 'but' statements or moments? How did you feel at the time? How would you now reword these?
   - Rewrite your 'but' statements using 'and' and put these in a safe place. Pull these out at least three times over the next two weeks and read them out aloud again.

CHAPTER FIVE | **HOW TO USE WORDS, METAPHORS AND ACTIONS TO AFFECT YOUR FEELINGS**

You may also care to discuss this technique with a good friend and both try the technique together – this can be a powerful (and often fun) learning experience.

Final comment:

If you still have some scepticism about how effective words can be in changing your feelings then perhaps changing your facial expressions might be a good place to start. It's known for instance that even fake smiles can affect your feelings. In a paper titled (you guessed it) "Grin and bear it", researchers Kraft and Pressman found that fake smiling both reduced the physical effect of stress on the body and improved recovery from stress. So, just "Grin and bear it"!

CHAPTER 6

How positive and negative words affect brain power

Can the words we use change the way our brain functions?

"Sticks and stones may break your bones, but words can never hurt you" – that's what the old nursery rhyme tells us. While we've always wanted to believe that words may not hurt us, can words make our brains healthier?

It seems so.

Recent research by Andrew Newberg and Mark Robert Waldman (*Words Can Change Your Brain*) suggests that certain words have an impact on specific areas of the brain. As discussed in Chapter 2, we've seen that positive words can affect our behaviour. This new research now shows why.

Positive words such as 'peace' and 'love' can alter what is known as 'the expression of genes'. Genes store information in our brain and act like a book, so the expression of genes occurs when the information in the book is accessed and communicated. When we use positive words they strengthen areas in our frontal lobes and promote the brain's cognitive functioning, making us more cognitively healthy. They propel the motivational centres of the brain into action, according to Newberg and Waldman, and build resiliency.

CHAPTER SIX | HOW POSITIVE AND NEGATIVE WORDS AFFECT BRAIN POWER

However, unlike the nursery rhyme premise, it seems that words can also hurt you. Newberg and Waldman's research points out five really important factors about how both positive and negative words affect our brain – this is particularly the case over extended periods. In summary:

1. By holding a positive and optimistic word in your mind, you stimulate frontal lobe activity. This area includes specific language centres that connect directly to the motor cortex responsible for moving you into action.
2. The longer you concentrate on positive words, the more you begin to affect other areas of the brain.
3. When using positive or negative words over an extended period, functions in the parietal lobe start to change, which alters your perception of yourself and the people you interact with.
4. A positive view of yourself will bias you towards seeing the good in others, whereas a negative self-image will lead you towards suspicion and doubt about others.
5. Finally over time, the structure of your thalamus will also change in response to your conscious words, thoughts and feelings. These thalamic changes affect the way in which you perceive reality.

In terms of improved 'brain power' there's also more evidence from an unlikely source – fiction writers. It seems as though reading fiction (regularly) can also improve our self-image and indeed empathy for others.

Researchers Mar, Oatley and Peterson report that individuals who frequently read fiction seem to be better able to understand other people, empathise with them and see the world from their perspective.

It seems that brain scans (through the use of functional Magnetic Resonance Imaging machines – fMRI machines) are revealing what happens in our brain when we read a detailed description, an evocative metaphor or an emotional exchange between characters. Stories stimulate the brain and even change how we act in life.

Researchers have long known that the 'classical' language regions, like Broca's area and Wernicke's area, are involved in how the brain interprets written words. What scientists have now come to realise is that narratives activate many other parts of our brains as well, suggesting why the experience of reading can feel so alive. Words like 'lavender', 'cinnamon' and 'soap' for example, elicit a response not only from the language-processing areas of our brains, but also those devoted to dealing with smells.

In fact scientists now posit that our sensors (such as eyes, ears, nose, mouth) are merely devices that send messages to many parts of the brain, not as was once thought to specific areas such as the language areas (i.e., Broca and Wernicke). In his bestselling book *The Brain That Changes Itself*, author Norman Doidge quotes neuroplasticity scientist Paul Bach-y-Rita as saying "We see with our brains, not with our eyes". The ability of injured or impaired people to learn to perceive senses such as sight, hearing, smell and touch through sensors other than those thought to be traditionally 'hardwired' to a particular sense is now further evidence that our brains can learn to change by the exercises we use to train them. Perhaps this knowledge may be additional motivation to try several of the exercises in this book.

You can quickly test this theory for yourself. Place your hand horizontally, with your palm facing upwards in front of you and imagine holding a lemon. Look at the lemon – see the yellow and green tones. Feel the lemon resting in the palm of your hand. Smell the fragrant citrus aroma. Your mouth will salivate as a response to the thought. Your conscious mind knows no lemon is present, but it is

CHAPTER SIX | HOW POSITIVE AND NEGATIVE WORDS AFFECT BRAIN POWER

sending signals to the parts of the brain that senses the sight, smell and taste of a lemon (as I write this I am actually salivating!)

In addition to the many 'brain-changing' breakthrough training techniques that are now helping to cure the sick or injured, or people who have been born with disabilities, our growing understanding of how the brain can be trained to change the way we act is useful for every one of us. For instance returning to the fiction example, Oatley notes, "Fiction is a particularly useful simulation because negotiating the social world effectively is extremely tricky, requiring us to weigh up myriad interacting instances of cause and effect. Just as computer simulations can help us get to grips with complex problems such as flying a plane or forecasting the weather, so novels, stories and dramas can help us understand the complexities of social life."

And long before fMRI machines were available to 'read our brains', psycholinguists were aware of the differences in cognitive complexity between expressing something in the positive as opposed to the negative. For example negation invariably leads to an increase in grammatical complexity which means it takes longer for the speaker to express and longer for the listener to interpret what is being said. Hear the difference between the following:

AFFIRMATIVE	NEGATIVE
The book is here.	The book is not here.
Ellen has some money.	Ellen doesn't have any money.
Tie	Untie
One	None

Just as when we discussed the difficulty for the listener when interpreting a 'don't' statement or question (i.e. the lack of visual imagery and the need for double processing), the difficulty is also evident in most all negations. For example, when the listener has to process "Ellen doesn't have any money" he or she has to conjure up the image of money; what it is, how much does she "not have?", and perhaps start thinking about "Why doesn't she have any?".

Intuitively too we know that negative phrasing and language often:

- Tells the other person what cannot be done
- Has a subtle tone of blame
- Includes words like don't, can't, won't, unable to, that demonstrates to the other person what you or they cannot do
- Does not stress positive actions that would be appropriate or positive consequences

And we also know that positive phrasing and language:

- Tells the other person what can be done
- Suggests alternatives and choices available to us and others
- Sounds helpful and encouraging
- Stresses positive actions and positive consequences

Now this final Chapter in Part One also provides conclusive evidence about what happens in our brain when we are using either positive or negative language. It shows the incredible power that words have on our thoughts, feelings and actions as they infiltrate various areas of our brain.

There are no 'Suggestions' or 'Next Steps' in this Chapter – I'll leave it to your intent and motivation to take the action you think may work best for you. To help you make those decisions, following is a brief summary of the key points from the first five Chapters.

PART ONE | HOW WORDS IMPACT OUR BEHAVIOUR

Summary – where are we now?

Chapter 1 **The 'don't' rule:**	Completely eliminate the word 'don't' from your vocabulary.	Think of what you would like (or want) people to do, and say so.
Chapter 2 **Eliminate negative words:**	Eliminate negative words from your conversation, emails, texts and other communication.	Replace these negative words with the positive alternative.
Chapter 3 **The 'Futureless Concept':**	Express the future as if it's already happening.	For example, express things you are going to do as "I am" rather than "I will", "I must", or "I want to".
Chapter 4 **Practise using metaphors:**	Use metaphors, particularly in your written communication.	Also, try using 'and' (with an appropriate pause) to uncover the true meaning or feeling behind what someone else is expressing when they use a metaphor.
Chapter 5 **Practise changing the descriptions of your negative feelings into words that are 'quirky':**	Change negative feelings into words that are more positive.	Better still, change negative words into metaphors that will enable you to lighten up the negativity you may feel in a challenging or difficult situation.

PART ONE | **HOW WORDS IMPACT OUR BEHAVIOUR**

A final comment:

As you've seen, one of the key themes in this book is to be more positive by using positive language. The unfortunate news is that there are more negatively oriented words than positively oriented words in our language to choose from. Linguists Robert Schrauf and Julia Sanchez (quoted in *The Man Who Lied to His Laptop* by Clifford Nass) have shown that in the two languages they studied – English and Spanish – only 20 per cent of words have a neutral orientation, 50 per cent have a negative orientation and the remaining 30 per cent have a positive orientation.

It comes as no surprise to me then that we (as a society) are inadvertently programming ourselves to be more negative by the amount of negative words we use and hear on a daily basis. And this starts at an early age. For instance it's been found that the average child hears 432 negative comments or words per day versus 32 positive ones. If my maths is correct that's about 93% negative! From that starting point it's little wonder that so much of our language is negative.

Now with the evidence presented here, you and I can start turning that figure around.

PART TWO
Words to use, words to avoid and other influencing factors when communicating

Introduction to Part 2

In Part 1 we saw how words can impact behaviour. Part 2 now moves from words to phrases to finally conversation. What are the best words and phrases to use to ensure your intent has the desired impact? What are some words or phrases to avoid that are recognised 'conversation busters'? Is there a defined process that allows you to navigate your way through the troubled waters of a difficult conversation? How can you actually manage a difficult conversation to achieve an effective outcome for both people?

All of these questions will be answered as we progress through Part 2. It has three Chapters:

PART TWO | WORDS TO USE, WORDS TO AVOID AND OTHER INFLUENCING FACTORS WHEN COMMUNICATING

Chapter 7, "Words or phrases that make difficult conversations even more difficult – How words can make or break a relationship" looks at the most common cause of difficult conversations (which can quite often end in conflict) – the word 'you'. It also looks at a phrase we learnt as young children and one that continues to cause us trouble as mature adults – 'yes but'. You'll be pleased to know that there are some very easy techniques for avoiding these two most unwelcome conversation busters.

Chapter 8, "The importance of tone of voice – Can words alone ensure our intended message has the desired impact?" introduces the method for applying what we've learnt from previous Chapters – the tone that we use when conversing. It shows how a simple change in the way we say a word or phrase can change the entire meaning. Once again there are some suggested exercises to show how this can be done (including one that's used by budding actors, so that could be fun!).

Chapter 9, "The process of a conversation – Can you actively manage a conversation?" takes the communication process one step further and talks about conversation. Do conversations meander aimlessly, whether they be idle chit chat, small talk, or even perhaps gossip, through to more serious relationship issues? Or is there a defined process that we all use whenever we have a conversation – be it a short morning catch-up or a more serious life changing discussion? All will be revealed in Chapter 9, which leads us nicely into Part 3.

In Part 3, we'll cover how to manage a range of difficult and challenging conversations. In the meantime read on to identify which words and phrases you currently use that should be thrown away and which ones you should pick up and treasure.

CHAPTER 7

Words or phrases which make difficult conversations even more difficult

Can words make or break a relationship?

The ubiquitous 'you'

Try to think back to the last difficult, conflicting or angry conversation you had with a loved one – where both of you became quite emotional. What was the cause? You may say it was a difference of opinion over a topic, and that's definitely partly true. My contention is that although you both differed in your opinions on the topic (or cause of the issue), it was not this difference that raised the conversation to an emotional level (or lowered it). Rather, it was the words that were used by either or more probably both of you as each put forward argument and counter argument.

Were there any swear words thrown around? Did it get as emotional as that? I'll wager that the word being thrown around more than any other and the one that caused the conversation to intensify into conflict was 'you' e.g. "You never do …", "You

PART TWO | **WORDS TO USE, WORDS TO AVOID AND OTHER INFLUENCING FACTORS WHEN COMMUNICATING**

always do/say that", "Why don't you …". Do any of these phrases ring any bells?

Look at the following example given by a bank supervisor to a teller (this was written on a performance review, so it is a real example):

"You are disorganised and as a result you don't get the work through on time. You don't seem to be really interested in getting the right results. You don't follow instructions at all well. You make too many silly mistakes in the balancing and I don't think you are really suited to the role of teller."

How would you feel if you were the teller? Notice again how many times the word 'you' is used:

"<u>You</u> are disorganised and as a result <u>you</u> don't get the work through on time. <u>You</u> don't seem to be really interested in getting the right results. <u>You</u> don't follow instructions at all well. <u>You</u> make too many silly mistakes in the balancing and I don't think <u>you</u> are really suited to the role of teller."

What sort of response did it bring? Well, here's the teller's reply:

"I am not disorganised. I keep my desk clean for the benefit of the customers. Any mistakes I make are quickly corrected. As for my being suitable for the role, I am very customer oriented. Any uncertainty I show is not because of my skills but because of the way instructions are given. If instructions were given in a positive way by you and not as criticism, then I would be better at my job."

Why does a simple word such as 'you' cause such problems?

Used in the past tense, it almost always infers blame or criticism (think back to your difficult conversation – was there blame, criticism?). For example:

- ***You*** *always do that to me.*
- ***You*** *never do anything I want.*
- *Why can't **you** do what I tell you?*

CHAPTER SEVEN | WORDS OR PHRASES WHICH MAKE DIFFICULT CONVERSATIONS EVEN MORE DIFFICULT

- *You are always late.*
- *You always make that mistake.*
- *You should not push so hard. It's rude and it gets everyone upset.*
- *You are always so messy – why can't **you** be tidy for a change?*

Have you heard about 'you' causing problems before? If not, it may seem a little strange; after all, we use 'you' practically every time we have a conversation, and not all conversations take a downward spiral into a dog fight.

Reading a LinkedIn posting recently by John Blakey, (an experienced CEO and Group Chair for Vistage) titled "8 Words to Avoid when Giving Feedback", he too felt the same way. Blakey was attending a training program for CEOs which included a session on giving feedback when the facilitator listed a number of words to avoid. Blakey writes, "It was the last two words that caught my eye. How can you possibly deliver feedback without using the words 'you' and 'your'? What purpose could there be in missing out these words? My colleagues in the group had similar reservations and a noisy debate struck up. Our facilitators brought the debate to a halt through a demonstration where they contrasted the following two pieces of feedback by saying:

- *When the classroom has discussions, you are not really paying attention or asking questions; it seems like you are pretty detached.*
- *In the classroom discussions, I have noticed not paying attention or asking questions; I wondered if this was detachment".*

The second piece of feedback was given without the use of 'you'. In fact rather than 'you' used in the first example to confront the entire class, the focus is now very clearly on the behaviour being displayed – "not paying attention or asking questions". This results in the participants focusing on their behaviour rather than perhaps being affronted as they may have been in the first piece of feedback.

Now getting rid of the problem word 'you' is difficult. It's very natural to say "You are not paying attention". So what do you replace it with? (Look for the clue in the second example given by the facilitators above – it appears twice).

To see how an alternative to 'you' might work, let's return to the bank teller and hear how she gave feedback to the supervisor who had just roundly criticised her:

"I am not disorganised. I keep my desk clean for the benefit of the customers. Any mistakes I make are quickly corrected. As for my being suitable for the role, I am very customer oriented. Any uncertainty I show is not because of my skills but because of the way instructions are given. If instructions were given in a positive way <u>by you</u> and not as criticism, then I would be better at my job."

This is a very good response. The teller replies in a confident, assertive manner and only uses 'you' once. In fact if the teller deleted the words "by you", her response would be perfect and would still make sense, without being confrontational.

So what do you replace 'you' with, and how can it work in practice?

The 'I' message

Notice that instead of using 'you' the teller has spoken from an 'I' perspective (the only mistake being "by you" on one occasion). Because the 'you' message implies criticism, when used as part of the feedback process it triggers the person's natural fight or flight defence mechanism. They either become quite angry or aggressive, or retreat into themselves. As a result they tend not to accept the feedback.

CHAPTER SEVEN | WORDS OR PHRASES WHICH MAKE DIFFICULT CONVERSATIONS EVEN MORE DIFFICULT

Let's focus for a moment on what happens in the brain when it hears the word 'you' followed by a critical comment. All information coming into the brain passes through the thalamus which classifies information in a binary manner – i.e., is this information good or bad? Safe or dangerous? If the thalamus decides it's 'safe' then it may get further processed elsewhere without causing any undue discomfort or stress. However, if the thalamus decides this information could be dangerous, then the brain automatically triggers the fight or flight defence mechanism and so it's easy to see why 'you' causes people to get upset so quickly – the brain is telling us "this information could be harmful – be wary, fight back or get out of here!"

Returning to the teller and her supervisor – could the message by the supervisor to the teller been given in a way that would have been accepted?

Yes. The answer is to avoid 'you' and use 'I' messages instead. Here's an approach the supervisor could have used:

"Sue, thanks for taking a moment of your time to talk with me. I'm new to the role of supervisor, so I feel a bit uncomfortable with this. Please bear with me. I've noticed over the last two weeks that the batch work has not been getting through on time. This seems unusual to me, as it's normally OK. Has anything changed over the last two weeks that might have led to these delays?"

Notice that as was the case with the John Blakey's training facilitators, the emphasis in the supervisor's new message is now squarely on the issue, not the teller. In this way both can discuss and focus quite rationally on solving the problem rather than debating and defending each other's words and actions.

Using 'I' messages is such an important rule, that below are some examples of how to change 'you' into 'I'. Next time you have to tell someone they are annoying you, or that they've upset you, or perhaps

PART TWO | **WORDS TO USE, WORDS TO AVOID AND OTHER INFLUENCING FACTORS WHEN COMMUNICATING**

that they've done something that concerns you, take a few moments to prepare your message. You can do this mentally or, better still (if you have time), by writing out what you intend to say as an 'I' message before you have the conversation.

The 'I' Message – Changing 'you' into 'I' …

'you' message …	'I' message …
You broke your promise	I felt let down
You never do anything that I want correctly.	I would like to see it done this way (or "another way").
You made me so angry because you forgot to give me a ride home.	I feel angry when I am expecting a ride home and I'm forgotten.
Why can't you do what I tell you?	I'd like my instructions followed please.
You always make that mistake.	It's disappointing to me that this mistake happens regularly.
You should not push so hard. It's rude and it gets everyone upset.	I get upset when I see people flinch sometimes during our conversations. My impressions are that they react negatively to the use of some words and phrases.
You are always so messy.	I feel disappointed because this mess has not been cleaned up.
You made a mistake.	That's incorrect. I'd like to see it done this way.
You should have called earlier.	I'd like to get a call in plenty of time so that I can …
Why didn't you call us when you found out about the changes?	I would like to hear about this sooner so that I can make the changes in plenty of time.

CHAPTER SEVEN | **WORDS OR PHRASES WHICH MAKE DIFFICULT CONVERSATIONS EVEN MORE DIFFICULT**

'you' message ...	'I' message ...
You shouldn't tell stories out of school.	I think telling stories that are not true about someone is unfair because others will believe the stories and dislike the person for the wrong reasons.
You have to fill out these forms.	I need to have these forms completed.
Your report was not handed in on time last week which made me look very stupid in the meeting.	I was disappointed that I did not get the report on time. This made it very hard for me during the meeting.
Your performance is not up to standard.	I'm disappointed that the performance standards we agreed on are not being met.
You have not met one of the key objectives we set at the start of the period.	I'm disappointed that all of the key objectives we set at the start of the period have been missed.

In fact 'you' is not just a poor way of getting our message across, it can actually be quite damaging to our relationships. Think for a moment about a recent conversation you've had where you disagreed on a topic or point. Now please keep that conversation in mind. How would you feel if the other person said one of the following to you?

Write one or two words to describe your feelings:
- *You neglected to ...*
- *You failed to ...*
- *You overlooked (or forgot) ...*

1. If someone said these to me I would feel

....

- *You claim that ...*
- *You say that ...*
- *You state that ...*

2. If someone said these to me I would feel

....

Don't — *How using the right words will change your life*

PART TWO | **WORDS TO USE, WORDS TO AVOID AND OTHER INFLUENCING FACTORS WHEN COMMUNICATING**

- *You should ...*
- *You ought to ...*
- *You must ...*

3. If someone said these to me I would feel

....

- *No doubt you will ...*
- *With respect, you should ...*
- *You understand of course that ...*

4. If someone said these to me I would feel

....

Read back over the words you have written. These are similar to the feelings everyone experiences when someone else directs a 'you' barb at us. Powerful (and potentially hurtful) aren't they?

I've done this exercise too and you can see my reactions at the back of the book. If you'd like some practice at changing 'you' to 'I', try doing so by rewording the above phrases into 'I' messages. I've also included my suggested changes for these at the back of the book.

The 'I' Message – Can you ever use 'you' in a difficult situation?

We've now seen how powerful, effective and positive 'I' messages are, but is there any danger in using 'I' messages?

Yes. They can seem manipulative if they are inappropriately combined with 'you'. For example "I feel unhappy that you are late" on the surface seems like a good 'I' message. While the words "I feel unhappy" are legitimate because they are expressing only your feelings, they become impotent and even blameful when the words "you are late" are added. In this case the person may now feel even more responsible for how you are feeling about their lateness – as a result they are most likely to become defensive.

The manipulative use of 'I' messages becomes particularly unproductive when there is a power or authority difference between the two people, for example when used by a parent with a child, a teacher with a student or a manager with an employee. We'll explore some of these with specific examples in Part 3.

The 'I' Message – Follow the 4 guidelines for using 'I' ...

The best way of ensuring that you get the 'I' message correct is to follow four simple guidelines:

1. **Describe the behaviour**, e.g. *"When people call me names ..."* – make sure the word 'you' is omitted – use only 'I', 'me', 'my' or 'mine'.
2. **Define the feeling it is causing**, e.g. *"I feel hurt"* – make sure it is only your feeling.
3. **Define the effect the behaviour has on you**, e.g. *"Because it starts to weaken my self-confidence"* – make sure it is only the impact it is having on you, not others (you can't speak for them).
4. **Use 'you' only in the future tense**, e.g. *"What can you do to help stop this name-calling?"* – note that 'you' is always used in a question about the future and is almost always a call for help.

So the total sentence from the above examples becomes:

"When people call me names I feel hurt because it starts to weaken my self-confidence. What can you do to help stop this name-calling?"

PART TWO | **WORDS TO USE, WORDS TO AVOID AND OTHER INFLUENCING FACTORS WHEN COMMUNICATING**

Please read the above sentence again. I trust that it shows that a constructive, non-blameful and supportive conversation is now likely to follow.

The 'I' Message – Are there any exceptions?

Can there be any exceptions to these guidelines? For example, is it possible to use 'you' in the present or past tense?

Using 'you' in the past tense as in "You've made that mistake a lot" is a definite no-no! Note here that we are talking about difficult conversations where our comment or opinion is likely to be negative or at the very least, something we or they will not like. In these cases 'you' used in the past tense will infer criticism or blame. So 'you' should only be used in the future tense. And it's almost always as a request for help, guidance or assistance. For example, "What can you do to help me get this place cleaned up?" We've seen the logic that, used in the past tense, 'you' can infer criticism or blame, but the future hasn't happened – we can't change the past but we can decide (together) on the future.

And while not quite as damaging as using 'you' in a critical way, it can also be less helpful when giving positive news. For example when we have a positive message to give it's advisable to avoid 'you' as rather than blame or criticism, it can cause embarrassment. For example it's easier for a person to accept praise when we say "I really like the way that project was completed – it was correct and on-time" rather than "You did a great job on that project". There's a separate Chapter in Part 3 on how to give praise that covers this in detail.

However, there is one exception to our guidelines, and that's for using 'you' in the present tense; but only in the present tense and only in some extenuating circumstances. For example, when we perceive that our partner, good friend or perhaps our child has a problem, the temptation is to say something like "What's wrong?" to which they will invariably respond "Nothing". One way of overcoming this barrier is to *use an 'I' message as a question*. For example, "I get the impression that you are unhappy. *Am I right?*" Although we have used a 'you', notice here that the emphasis is now on our "impression" – "Am I right?" It is now most likely that the other person will respond by opening up and talking about their unhappiness – or at the very least, they are likely to tell you why they are not unhappy – and so you move into a conversation rather than receiving a blunt "Nothing". And it's because we've used 'you' in the present tense and as a non-threatening 'I-question' that 'you' becomes acceptable.

The 'I' Message – and what about 'we' – can we use 'we' instead of 'you'?

Often people suggest they can see the logic of not using 'you' and so they use 'we' instead, which they believe will soften the ensuing statements. Does this succeed?

Well, I can vividly recall a difficult conversation I was having many years ago with my partner. I can't recall the topic and only clearly remember her response after I said "I think we have a problem". She replied "We have a problem?" – with great emphasis on the **WE** and it was definitely not used as a rhetorical question! Being a sensitive person, I got her message straight away. She was in fact saying WE don't have a problem, YOU do (meaning me).

In this instance I had used 'we' illegitimately. It's easy to see why my partner reacted so snappishly to my simple statement as 'we' had not agreed on the problem nor its likely cause.

Can 'we' be used constructively?

Yes, 'we' can be used – but only when both parties have agreed on the cause or reasons for the issue/problem. That is both people understand very clearly what the problem is, and/or the reasons why it has arisen and the fact that they are both going to work hard at fixing it. So it is now a shared problem and both people can legitimately use 'we'.

In fact a study at the University of California, Berkeley has found that the use of 'we' more often than 'I' in conversations (between spouses) has been shown to indicate the strength of a marriage relationship. "The use of 'we' language is a natural outgrowth of a sense of partnership, of being on the same team, and confidence in being able to face problems together," said study co-author Benjamin Seider. Keep in mind the caveat that the problem or likely cause must first be agreed.

The rules for using 'I', 'you' and 'we' in difficult (or potentially difficult) conversations are:

- 'I' should be used at all times to express an opinion, feeling or describe feedback to another person. 'I' messages should replace 'you' messages.
- 'You' should only be used in the future tense. We can't change the past, we can influence the future, e.g. "What can you do to help?"
- 'We' can only be used when both parties agree on the key issue or point of difference.

In a difficult conversation, the order of using these three words generally becomes:
1. "**I** have a problem/issue/concern. This is how **I** see things ..."
2. "How do **YOU** see it?" or "How can **YOU** help?" (depending on the issue and situation)

CHAPTER SEVEN | WORDS OR PHRASES WHICH MAKE DIFFICULT CONVERSATIONS EVEN MORE DIFFICULT

3. "What can **WE** do to work through this issue?" (once both people have agreed, and only when they've agreed that there is an issue or problem)

Note: You'll soon find out in a conversation if you jump too quickly to the 'we' – the other party will most likely contradict you, or they'll retreat into themselves as they know that the problem has yet to be defined and agreed to by both people.

'But' and 'yes, but'

As with 'you', 'but' is another word we use regularly. When used by one person to describe two alternatives, for example I might say, "At first glance the EasyGo washing machine looks like the better choice for us – it's cheaper and is used by a lot of people. But when the BestGo machine is compared in detail to EasyGo it shines in most categories with the exception of price." As there is only one person involved and putting two alternative points of view, 'but' works very well.

It's when 'but' is used by one person in conversation to counter the argument or point being made by another that 'but' runs into trouble and gets its bad name. Quite often what follows the 'but' is a criticism of the point being made by the other person, or a criticism of the person. In fact it quite often starts out as 'but' and then escalates to:

- "But, don't you think ..."
- "But wouldn't it be best to ..."
- "But why should we do that?"
- "But why would anyone make that choice?"

In fact we've probably become culturally acclimatised to expect criticism every time someone starts a sentence with the 'but' tone of voice. For example, "I really liked the way you cooked the stir fry, but I found it a bit too sweet". Despite the sentence starting with the good news, we instinctively seem to know that the 'but' is coming.

And then there's 'yes, but'.

At first glance, 'yes, but' could be seen as better than 'but', yet it gives a very mixed message – is the person agreeing with your idea and then putting an alternative? Most often not. They are probably trying to be courteous or kind when contradicting your idea or point. It doesn't work. People still only hear the 'but" – and what follows the 'but' – and the 'yes' becomes meaningless.

For instance, have you ever experienced a time when someone says "Yes, I get that" and you feel quite pleased. And then they follow up with something like, "Yes, but it will never work".

'Yes, but' makes difficult conversations even more difficult because if used regularly it's heard as a constant stream of criticism. If used a lot by one person, the other stops listening. If used a lot by both people, they not only stop listening but use the speaker's time to think about their own next 'yes, but' (and often talk over the speaker or interject too early with their point).

How do you counter 'yes, but' and what can it be replaced with?

Some people have suggested using 'but's' first cousins 'however' or 'although'. These however, are just a polite form of 'but'. They do not have quite the critical impact, but still provide the speaker with the lead in to his or her counter argument and at the same time cause the receiver to stop listening, merely spinning their wheels waiting to jump in with their own 'but', 'however' or 'although'.

And there's another very good reason for replacing 'but' for it gives mixed messages. Using 'but' or 'yes, but' tells the other person

CHAPTER SEVEN | WORDS OR PHRASES WHICH MAKE DIFFICULT CONVERSATIONS EVEN MORE DIFFICULT

you've either not believed a thing they said before or you totally disagree with their point.

A very good way of replacing 'yes, but' is to say instead 'yes, and'. Using this technique has proven to be a fantastic way of enriching the original idea.

'Yes, and' is used in many personal communication, conflict resolution and negotiation training programs. It's also used as an improvisation tool by actors and directors developing themes for the theatre where each idea builds on the previous idea by saying "Yes, and how about …?"

Although in a conversation you may have a different opinion from the one being put forward, 'yes, and' forces you to think about the point being made by the other person, postpone your judgment and then add to their idea, thus making the conversation rich and constructive. In this way both people can fully explore the issue and all the options in a harmonious way. 'Yes, and' also gives you a natural opportunity to talk about your interests and move the conversation back to an area where you're more likely to find common ground.

So for example if you find you have to negotiate with your boss at work over extended hours, using the 'yes, and' technique you might say, "Yes, and I would like you to be able to rely on me at all times. And I have two small children for whom I need to be home at 6pm every day. If anything urgent comes up after that time I will respond via email or Skype after 7pm. How does that sound?"

Please keep in mind that 'but' and 'however' are quite OK when one person is using them to compare two points or perhaps different perspectives – it's when they are used to counter the points being made by others in conversation that they can cause problems.

So, there you have it –

PART TWO | **WORDS TO USE, WORDS TO AVOID AND OTHER INFLUENCING FACTORS WHEN COMMUNICATING**

The 'I', 'you', 'we' rules:

1. "**I** have a problem/issue/concern. This is how **I** see things …"
2. "How do **YOU** see it?" or "How can **YOU** help?" (depending on the issue and situation)
3. "What can **WE** do to work through this issue?"

and the 'yes, and' technique:

4. Replace 'but' and 'yes, but' with 'yes, and'.

We'll apply these rules and techniques throughout Part 3 – Difficult Conversations. In addition to the 'don't' rule, they apply to every difficult conversation you are likely to have.

Final comments:

Before we exit this Chapter, it's worth looking at a few more phrases that can cause problems. The results are not quite as disastrous as the inappropriate use of 'you' and 'but', but using these phrases is often seen as insincere and could either end the conversation (as meaningless) or at worst catapult it into the difficult category, so it's worth being wary about their use.

I'm referring to some of the phrases that are often taught in reflective listening courses. In essence, there's nothing wrong with reflective listening – used well and carefully it can be an effective communication skill – although there are many times when the 'and …' technique of Clean Language discussed in Chapter 4 can be far more effective.

The core principle on which reflective listening is built is that the person listening must be sincere. Some of the phrases that were

CHAPTER SEVEN | WORDS OR PHRASES WHICH MAKE DIFFICULT CONVERSATIONS EVEN MORE DIFFICULT

originally developed many years ago as 'summary stems' to ensure the listener summarised what was being heard, have now, through overuse or inappropriate use, lost their effectiveness and can often be seen as insincere. For example one that has become quite hackneyed and turns many people off is, "I hear what you're saying" (often followed by 'but'). For example when one person says, "I hear what you say" they often mean, "I hear what you say but I disagree with it so totally that I am not even going to bother considering it. In fact I have already forgotten it. Here's what I think …"

In his excellent article "I hear what you're saying but I'll ignore it" Miles Kington combined some of the common negative conversation busters (such as 'yes but') with ineffectual or overused reflective listening phrases to pen the following list of phrases to avoid (note that his article was written in 1996 and most if not all the phrases are still being used inappropriately today):

- "Yes but …"
- "That's all very well but …"
- "That may well be so but …"
- "Yes, I catch your drift, but …"
- "I can see where you're heading but …"
- "I take on board what you say."
- "Even assuming that to be the case …"
- "You may well be right but …"
- "With respect …"
- "With the greatest respect …"
- "I see what you mean …"
- "I see what you're getting at …"
- "I think I can see what you're driving at."
- "Nevertheless …"
- "Notwithstanding …"

PART TWO | **WORDS TO USE, WORDS TO AVOID AND OTHER INFLUENCING FACTORS WHEN COMMUNICATING**

- "Still and all …"
- "Mutatis mutandis …"
- "Other things being equal …"
- "So what you're saying is …"
- "I take your point, but …"
- "The point, surely, is that …"
- "We mustn't forget that …"
- "What we have to remember is that …"
- "What it all comes back to …"
- "This doesn't alter the fact that …"
- "We mustn't lose sight of the fact that …"
- "When all is said and done …"
- "At the end of the day …"
- "When the chips are down …"
- "What it's really all about …"
- "In the real world …"

Seen some that you are still using? Embarrassing isn't it! As a result of reading this list, I've now just dropped some. If you're using some of these I'd suggest making a note to change them to a more positive phrase – a simple 'yes, and' will probably cover most – and delete from your repertoire others that are really superfluous.

Some suggestions for trying out the 'I' messages rule and the 'yes, and …' technique …

1. Pick either the 'I' message rule or the 'Yes, and …' technique to focus on at one time.

CHAPTER SEVEN | WORDS OR PHRASES WHICH MAKE DIFFICULT CONVERSATIONS EVEN MORE DIFFICULT

2. Spend several days listening to the conversation of others as they discuss a point or issue. In particular, if you are going to focus on improving your 'I' messages, listen to the number of times 'you' is being used, or if your focus is 'Yes, and ...' the number of 'buts' being expressed by each party. Avoid practising at this stage, merely listen and observe – become an expert! Oh, and by the way, please try to conceal that wry smile when you recognise what is happening – it could well be mistaken and *you* may become the target of their differences.
3. Before you start practising, share your goal with a friend or two. You may well discover that he or she is also interested in trying these techniques; the exercise then becomes something you can both try.
4. After a few days of observation, you will be ready to start. Read the notes in this Chapter again. Then try to think about some non-threatening or non-consequential conversations or situations where you can practise.
5. As has been suggested in earlier exercises, ask one of your friends to give you a signal (say, a raised eyebrow, or a certain word) every time you slip up. This will increase your awareness of the old habit and eventually short-circuit it.
6. Leave yourself some reminders of the shift in phrasing you want to make around your home or office. For example, put a Post-it note on your day planner (or an entry in your diary) that says, "When I meet with Ann today for coffee, I'm only using 'I' and see how it goes".
7. If you'd like to take the practice a step further, record yourself re-running or practising some of the phrases from one of your conversations yesterday (where it may not have worked so well), only this time use the new rule or technique. The idea is

to become comfortable with the new phrasing. This could be particularly important in the case of 'Yes, and …' as it may seem a little awkward at first. Also, replacing 'you' with 'I' does take a fair bit of practice.
8. Now if you'd like to go even further with your practice, enrol one or two of your friends to role-play some situations with you. Although it may seem uncomfortable at first, I've found this exercise to be particularly helpful.
9. Remind yourself regularly – aloud – to reinforce the message to your brain. For example, "I am using more I-messages particularly when I'm giving a difficult message". (As an aside, notice here the phrasing "I am using …" rather than "I am going to …" from the earlier Chapter on using present tense to ensure change happens).
10. Be patient. It takes about three to four weeks to change a behaviour so keep up the regular practice.

Note: Use the same exercise if you want to try getting rid of some of the 'conversation busters' or 'insincere listening summaries' that you earlier identified from your daily conversations.

And do please keep in mind that any changes you decide to make will take time, patience and practice as they are probably changing a lifetime of existing habits.

Finally, Part Three outlines a number of conversations that are naturally difficult or can become difficult. In Part Three I'll be outlining how the rules for 'you' to be replaced with 'I', the 'Yes, and …' technique and eliminating some of the conversation busters, can work wonders when trying to navigate the blustery weather of a difficult conversation storm.

CHAPTER 8

The importance of tone of voice

Can words alone ensure our message has the desired impact?

So far we've emphasised using certain words and avoiding others – but is this enough to make our communication effective? In order to communicate the meaning of the message we want to send and its intent, it's also important to match the tone of voice to the words. Our message can be quite easily misinterpreted when the tone doesn't match the words (and also of course when our facial expressions say something different again). For example, let's return to the sentence used earlier in the book;

I did not say she stole the money.

Please read it aloud (that will definitely give you the tone of the message). Listening to your own voice, what's the intent of this seemingly very clear message?

Before proceeding take a moment to write down what you believe is the intent of this message.

Now read aloud each of the following statements placing emphasis in your tone on the underlined words:

PART TWO | WORDS TO USE, WORDS TO AVOID AND OTHER INFLUENCING FACTORS WHEN COMMUNICATING

<u>I</u> did not say she stole the money
I <u>did not</u> say she stole the money
I did not <u>say</u> she stole the money
I did not say <u>she</u> stole the money
I did not say she <u>stole</u> the money
I did not say she stole <u>the money</u>

As was suggested earlier, there are at least six different meanings for this simple sentence, depending on where you place the emphasis:

Sentence	Meaning or intent
<u>I</u> did not say she stole the money	It wasn't I who said she stole the money.
I <u>did not</u> say she stole the money	I definitely did not say she stole the money.
I did not <u>say</u> she stole the money	I didn't "say" she stole the money – I may have inferred it. However, I didn't say so.
I did not say <u>she</u> stole the money	It wasn't she who stole the money.
I did not say she <u>stole</u> the money	She may have borrowed the money, but did not steal it.
I did not say she stole <u>the money</u>	She did not steal the money – however she may have taken something else.

Waldman and Newberg point out in *Words Can Change Your Brain*, that the tone of voice is equally as important as the words used, when it comes to understanding what a person is really trying to convey. Add facial expressions to that and the listener can be put in quite a quandary as to what is really being communicated. For instance if when speaking a sentence the facial expression expresses one emotion, but the tone conveys a different one, neural or cognitive dissonance (the mental

CHAPTER EIGHT | THE IMPORTANCE OF TONE OF VOICE

stress or discomfort experienced by an individual who holds two or more contradictory beliefs, ideas, or values at the same time) takes place in the brain of the listener, causing him/her some confusion. The result? Trust erodes, suspicion increases, and cooperation decreases.

So it's not just <u>what</u> you say that matters, how you say it is equally important. This is particularly relevant whenever your message is in any way emotional. Your message (the words) is what you're trying to communicate. Your tone of voice is how you communicate. Tone takes a statement and either breathes life into it or sucks the life out of it. Tone is also relevant when trying to interpret or understand someone else's underlying emotions which they may not be expressing in words.

Often because of the emotion or lack of emotion in the topic or issue, our tone changes subconsciously. That's human nature – it's always going to happen from time to time. However, we can and should become more aware of, and quite adept at, using tone to more accurately convey the intent of our message.

You can practise your tone by undertaking exercises like those below where stressing certain words changes the feeling of what you're saying. Once again, please say these aloud as that's the only way you will be able to discern your tone.

Read aloud the following sentence, "What would you like me to do about it?" You'll see that it changes in feeling, meaning, and tone when you:

- Say it defensively (by emphasising the words 'would you')
    - "What **would you** like me to do about it?"
- Say it with curiosity (by emphasising the words 'like me')
    - "What would you **like me** to do about it?"
- Say it with apathy (by not emphasising any of the words, merely speaking in a monotone)
    - "What would you like me to do about it?"

PART TWO | WORDS TO USE, WORDS TO AVOID AND OTHER INFLUENCING FACTORS WHEN COMMUNICATING

At this point some readers may be thinking, "Ah yes, that's all very well and good, but I've heard that most of the message in our communication is conveyed non-verbally by our facial expressions." In fact for many decades, communication and management trainers have built their lessons on communication around the theory that:

- 55% of one's message is conveyed by facial expressions,
- 38% by tone of voice,
- 7% by the actual words used.

However, those percentages are in fact a myth. I have to put my hand up here and admit that I too peddled this theory in my early days as a management trainer.

They are supposedly based on the research conducted and published by Professor Albert Mehrabian in 1967 and quoted out of context. In fact Mehrabian himself says, "Please note that this and other equations regarding relative importance of verbal and nonverbal messages were derived from experiments dealing with communications of feelings and attitudes (i.e., like-dislike). *Unless a communicator is talking about their feelings or attitudes, these equations are not applicable"* (italics are my emphasis).

Mehrabian's formula was based in most part on two of his simple experiments where he asked participants to judge the feelings of a speaker by listening to a recording of a single word spoken in different tones of voice. That's right, one single word, not even a sentence!

In the first study, the participants had to rate the feelings of the speaker after listening to each of nine different words – three conveying liking (honey, dear and thanks), three conveying neutrality (maybe, really and oh) and three conveying disliking (don't, brute and terrible).

CHAPTER EIGHT | THE IMPORTANCE OF TONE OF VOICE

The words spoken were often inconsistent with the tone of voice used. For example, the word 'brute' when spoken in a positive tone (two female speakers were used on all nine words) or the word 'dear' when spoken in a negative tone. Each time the subjects had to make a rating on just the single word they had listened to.

In the second study, only one word was used. It was chosen to be as neutral as possible; the word was 'maybe'. Subjects listened to a recording of the word 'maybe' said in three tones of voice to convey liking, neutrality and disliking. At the same time they were shown photos of different facial expressions (photos were in black and white and all faces were female) and were asked to guess the emotions of the speaker.

To reiterate, Mehrabian's findings were that the non-verbal element of facial expressions and the tone of voice were more accurate communicators only when the speaker was communicating feelings and attitudes and are not applicable to communication in general. He was in fact looking at the resolution of inconsistent messages between words and feelings.

In an email to Max Atkinson published in Atkinson's book *Lend Me Your Ears* Mehrabian says, "I am obviously uncomfortable about misquotes of my work. From the very beginning I have tried to give people the correct limitations of my findings. Unfortunately the field of self-styled 'corporate image consultants' or 'leadership consultants' has numerous practitioners with very little psychological expertise."

So where does that leave us? How important are facial expressions, tone of voice and words?

As many writers have suggested:

> "If the figures of 55%, 38% and 7% are to be believed, I wouldn't need to buy headphones on a plane when watching movies."

PART TWO | WORDS TO USE, WORDS TO AVOID AND OTHER INFLUENCING FACTORS WHEN COMMUNICATING

> *"If only 7% of the message can be attributable to the words, then it would be very easy to learn to communicate in a foreign language."*
>
> *"If you've ever played charades, you'll know that words and language are by far the most effective way of expressing complex and abstract ideas."*
>
> *"How could a blind person communicate effectively if it were not for the words and tone of voice used?"*

Additionally, Dr. C.E. Johnson points out in an article "Debunking the "55%, 38%, 7% myth", just how important words are:

> *"Words and language are probably the primary motivation factors for human beings and they can be enhanced by proper congruent tonality and body language. They can also be somewhat diminished by incongruencies which then often show up as confusion and bewilderment in relationship situations. For example, think how often some battered women have desperately believed the words of their batterers despite overwhelming incongruent behavior. 'He said he was really going to change this time.'"*

That's the anecdotal stuff. The hard science also supports these writers who emphasise the importance of words and tone in all our communications (for an excellent summary of this research see "Brain scan sheds light on secret of speech" Ian Sample, *The Guardian* 3 Feb 2004).

Chapter 5 showed how important words are and how they impact certain areas of the brain. So yes, the words in any communication are very important – after all, sophisticated language is one of the key differences between humans and animals. But so too is *tone*, as tone can change the meaning of a word, phrase or sentence. When describing his research on tone, Dr. Tobias Grossmann of the Centre for Brain and Cognitive Development at the University of London said:

CHAPTER EIGHT | THE IMPORTANCE OF TONE OF VOICE

"Another important question addressed in this study was whether activity in infants' voice-sensitive brain regions is modulated by emotional prosody. Prosody, essentially the 'music' of speech, can reflect the feelings of the speaker, thereby helping to convey the context of language. In humans, sensitivity to emotional prosody is crucial for social communication. The researchers observed that a voice-sensitive region in the right temporal cortex showed increased activity when 7-month-old infants listened to words spoken with emotional (angry or happy) prosody. Such a modulation of brain activity by emotional signals is thought to be a fundamental brain mechanism to prioritize the processing of significant stimuli in the environment."

A suggested exercise for improving your tone

If you'd like to practise using tone of voice effectively, try the following exercise. Note: this exercise can be more powerful if you record and play back your voice, or better still involve a friend to provide feedback on your accuracy and together play back your voice.

For each of the following statements, try saying them with three different tones:

1. Happy
2. Excited
3. Angry

- *Good morning, how are you today?*
- *I like the idea you had about the new curtains.*
- *You did a really good job on fixing that broken step.*
- *I'd like to talk to you for a minute if this is a good time.*

PART TWO | **WORDS TO USE, WORDS TO AVOID AND OTHER INFLUENCING FACTORS WHEN COMMUNICATING**

- Would you like to go out for lunch tomorrow at 12 o'clock?
- I think that we should go with Jane's idea for the play.
- You make a good point, and I will keep that in mind.
- Could we talk about that a little later?
- It's really good to see you.
- Thank you for the compliment.

A final comment:

Tone of voice is so important to ensure the words are heard in the right context and have the impact that is intended, that all actors practise tone a great deal. For example one exercise they are given is to say the question "Where is the car?" imagining they are:

- Coming out of a shop and finding the car-park is empty
- Coming out of a shop and finding the car-park is full
- Showing a picture to a five-year-old
- Speaking to a teenage son/daughter

Try these for yourself to gauge the importance of tone. I'm sure you'll find the exercise quite stimulating and also perhaps a bit of fun – remember, you have to imagine yourself in these situations and then say "Where is the car?" (This could also be fun to try with your partner or friend – maybe there's an actor inside you waiting to get out.)

CHAPTER 9

The process of a conversation

Can you actively manage a conversation?

"Hello Alice, I'm Bob. Nice to meet you. (pause) *So what do you do?*" I asked as a conversation starter when meeting Alice at a party.

"*I'm a banker, specialising in foreign exchange,*" she replied.

"*Sounds interesting – do you enjoy it?*"

Alice hesitated for a moment or two – to me she seemed somewhat uninspired by her profession. "*It's pretty interesting, and I'll have a good lifestyle after I've been there a few years,*" she answered.

At this point I had two options. I could continue the drudgery of the normal conversation and go on talking about her job (by which she seemed less than totally enthused), or I could reframe the conversation and try to build a deeper emotional connection. I decided on the latter.

"*Sounds like a good plan. And what do you do that you're truly passionate about?*"

At first Alice seemed a bit confused, and I wondered if she'd always considered herself enthusiastic about banking, but then she gathered herself and responded, "*You know, I actually love the idea of starting a corporate design business one day.*"

So far in this book I've used the term 'communication' in a general sense to describe many interactions. However, 'conversation' becomes a far more specific form of communication. For example you can communicate by sending an email or text, leaving a voice mail on someone's phone, writing an article or even accessing data from the internet. Conversation, on the other hand, requires interaction between at least two people, and that's where the challenges start.

Conversations can be funny things – we start out somewhere and may end up at a totally different destination from the one we expected (for example, my conversation with Alice went somewhere that I did not expect). "How was your day?" is another conversation starter used by millions of people around the world when they meet up again at the end of the day – spouse to spouse, partner to partner, parent to child, and so on. What sort of responses do you get when you ask this question? Have you ever been surprised by the answers?

Conversations may seem quite unstructured and even aimless, yet they've been found to have a certain structure or process that people unknowingly follow. Later in this Chapter, I'll outline a 'Conversation Process' you can learn and follow whenever you may be faced with some of the difficult conversations covered in Part 3 of this book. I'll also cover some of the words, phrases and questions that can dramatically alter the nature and outcome of your conversations.

First, let's look at some of the components of a conversation. Hugh Dubberly writing in *What is conversation? How can we design for effective conversation?* lists six tasks that conversation participants must undertake. As you read these please think about a recent conversation you've had, for example at a party with friends or new acquaintances (such as mine with Alice), with your spouse/partner, perhaps a child or colleague. The reason for asking you to think about a recent conversation is that it will make the conversation tasks discussed here 'real' (your recent conversation doesn't have to

CHAPTER NINE | THE PROCESS OF A CONVERSATION

be a difficult one, any one will do). As you read through the six, I'll be asking:
- How did each of these six tasks occur?
- Who said what?
- Can you visualise or perhaps now realise when each task was undertaken or completed?

Now, what's the conversation you will be recalling?

Here are the six tasks Dubberly identified, together with my brief explanations and questions for you to consider:

1. Open a Channel: the speaker says something that is comprehensible to the listener. This may seem basic, but is essential. The situation must also seem comfortable, or at least non-threatening.
    - For example if the speaker says something in a language you don't understand or you can't hear what was said because of other noise, then a conversation does not start.
    - In your recent conversation, why did it seem easy to continue?

2. Commit to Engage: The listener must participate if only by continuing to listen. He/she is only likely to continue if they see value in the conversation.
    - In your recent conversation what value did you see in continuing the conversation, i.e. Why did you continue?
    - What value do you think the other person saw in the conversation?
    - Why did the conversation end? Was this too soon, too long or about right?

PART TWO | **WORDS TO USE, WORDS TO AVOID AND OTHER INFLUENCING FACTORS WHEN COMMUNICATING**

3. Construct Meaning: The people are able to understand one another through previous conversations, shared knowledge, common language or social norms.
   - What did the two of you share or have in common? How did you discover this shared meaning?
   - Were there specific questions either you or your partner asked that facilitated a shared understanding?

4. Converge on Agreement: People share some understanding of the topic even if minimal, or a desire to understand it if the conversation is to continue (although they may totally disagree on one another's reasons, logic, philosophy and so on). As a result of this shared understanding they will start to move towards an agreement, or at least an 'agreement to disagree'.
   - What did the two of you agree on, or perhaps 'agree to disagree' on?

5. Evolve: Either or both people are different after the conversation – this may be in their actions, beliefs or even a strengthening of their initial thoughts and ideas.
   - What did the conversation identify, confirm or change for you?
   - How did you feel following the conversation? Was this a different feeling from the one you had before?

6. Act or Transact: Either or both people do something as a result of the conversation – this may range from undertaking some action, telling someone else, or continuing to think (consciously) about the topic.

CHAPTER NINE | THE PROCESS OF A CONVERSATION

- What have you done since the conversation (that was related)?
- Who have you told about the conversation? Why?

Now during a challenging conversation, it will be nigh on impossible to remember all six tasks required to bring it to a satisfactory conclusion. After all, you will be totally immersed in the content, and rightly so. Remembering to complete these tasks will therefore be particularly challenging when your conversation is emotionally charged. So it will be useful to have some clear signposts to help you manage the process and progress to a satisfactory destination. The diagram on the next page may be a useful map to follow.

Note: Here I've introduced the words 'content' and 'process'. In conversations these are important concepts to understand and manage. The content is what the discussion is all about – the problems, issues, challenges. People in all difficult or challenging conversations become heavily engrossed in the content. The process on the other hand, is how the conversation is managed – the questions, summaries, timing, format. When difficult conversations end in an impasse, devolve into argument or just fail to reach any conclusions, it's almost always because the people are so focussed on the content and no-one is managing the process.

It's by being a good process manager that you can dramatically improve the way you manage difficult conversations. The following map is a good example of process management:

PART TWO | **WORDS TO USE, WORDS TO AVOID AND OTHER INFLUENCING FACTORS WHEN COMMUNICATING**

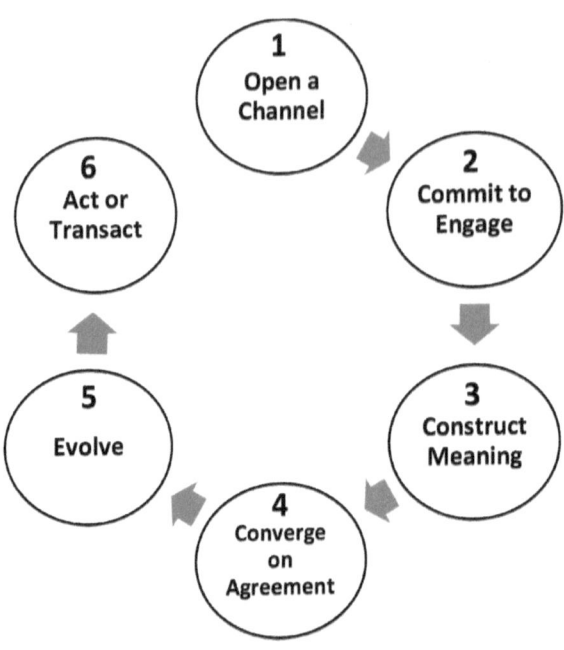

However, as Simon Garrod and Martin Pickering point out in *Why is conversation so easy?* there are other process issues that can challenge the fluidity of a conversation:

> *"Conversation (also) presents a whole range of interface challenges. These include deciding when it is socially appropriate to speak, being ready to come in at just the right moment (on average we start speaking about 0.5 seconds before our partner finishes), planning what you are going to say while still listening to your partner, and, in multi-party conversations, deciding who to address. To do this you have to keep task-switching (one moment speaking, the next moment listening). Yet we know that in general multi-tasking and task switching are really challenging – try writing a letter while listening to someone talking to you."*

CHAPTER NINE | THE PROCESS OF A CONVERSATION

Nevertheless the scientific research tells us there is good news too! In addition to being able to use the Process Map for conversations, there is a natural phenomenon that makes all conversations a little easier – it's known as 'interactive alignment'. People do this by making use of each other's choices of words, sounds, grammatical forms and meanings. The scientific reason for this is that interactive alignment occurs because the speaker activates linguistic representations in the listener's brain that are common to him/her. When responding, the listener (subconsciously) then speaks in ways that the other person will understand.

You will also recall from Chapter 4 that using metaphors is a way of providing common meaning for people in conversation – these too are a form of interactive alignment. As Raymond W. Gibbs points out in *The Cambridge Handbook of Metaphor and Thought*, "Much of our reasoning makes use of conceptual metaphors."

The function of interactive alignment is why it's so important to choose the most appropriate words for the content, context and for managing the process of a particularly difficult conversation. In doing so, the other participant or participants are more likely to follow your lead.

It's also been found that not only do we align linguistically with the other person in a conversation, we actually mirror their facial expressions. Commonly known as 'mirroring' the scientific term is 'emotional contagion', that is we instinctively synchronise our facial expressions with those of others. Watch people who are in animated conversations and their mannerisms and even voice tonal qualities will start to become similar. Note that this also occurs even when they are in disagreement about the context or content of the conversation, provided both are fully engaged in the conversation and not looking for 'a way out'. Amazingly, it's been found that some people with severely impaired vision or who may be clinically blind also exhibit emotional contagion.

So with the knowledge of the naturally occurring interactive alignment and mirroring, and armed with a good process map, our difficult conversations can now be more easily managed. Following are some suggestions for how to use these.

1. Open a Channel: The speaker says something that is comprehensible to the listener. Think of this as a 'discussion space' that opens up possibilities and helps both people make good decisions. In a difficult conversation it may take some time to get this space going but it's worth persevering. This discussion space may be:

- An actual physical setting, such as a comfortable area with tea/coffee/water etc.
- The way you stand or sit. For example, it's known that it's easier for people to remain calm when they are sitting rather than standing, or as we'll see in a later Chapter for parents to talk with their teenage children side-by-side (as in going for a walk or sitting in the car) rather than directly face-to-face.
- Most importantly, the manner in which you make it easy for the other person to be open in what they say and how they feel – perhaps with your words or your inclination to listen (see more of this below).

2. Commit to Engage: The listener must participate if only by continuing to listen. He/she is only likely to continue if they see value in the conversation. Basically this is how well the other person (or people if there are more than one in the conversation) perceives you as a good listener – they feel they have something in common with you.

CHAPTER NINE | THE PROCESS OF A CONVERSATION

I'll make an assumption here – perhaps dangerous for an author – that you are familiar with the concept and skill of 'reflective listening'. Perhaps you've even done some training in this technique.

Reflective listening is a good communication tool. However, the overriding principle is that the listener must be sincere (you'll recall in an earlier Chapter where the overuse or misuse of paraphrasing can actually mitigate effective dialogue). When listening reflectively the listener wants to really hear what the other is saying and most importantly, the feelings he/she is either consciously or unconsciously expressing. Now that's a tall order!

If you consider yourself an effective reflective listener, then please continue using these techniques. If you'd like to take your listening skills to the next level then I'd suggest developing the Clean Language of 'and …' and 'yes, and …' that was mentioned in Chapter 4 (further suggested reading on Clean Language is outlined in the References section at the end of this book).

Above all, the one thing that will demonstrate your willingness to engage in and help you through any challenging conversation is *the ability to listen*; to listen to:

- **facts** – logic, reasoning
- **feelings** – attitudes, emotions

and to be able to distinguish between the two.

Examining the distinction between facts and feelings is relevant before we go on. All difficult conversations have an emotional undertone – for example, giving someone critical feedback; asking the boss for a raise; telling your teenage son that he cannot go out with his friends this evening, and so on. Although all of these examples are based on facts, that is 'feedback – the poor behaviour', 'the raise – an amount of

PART TWO | **WORDS TO USE, WORDS TO AVOID AND OTHER INFLUENCING FACTORS WHEN COMMUNICATING**

money' and 'your reasons why your son cannot go out'. It's how both people **feel** about the **facts** that make the conversation difficult.

This is a very important distinction.

There are some conversations in which you will want to focus on feelings (perhaps yours and theirs or just yours or specifically theirs) whereas in other conversations you will need to keep the conversation rational and fact-based. This distinction and when to focus on each will be discussed as we look at each of the challenging conversations in Part 3.

Are there words that can help focus the conversation on either facts or feelings?

Yes: Two of the most common are 'think' and 'feel'. When asking someone "What do you **think** about …?" they will invariably give you an explanation of their reasoning or logic. When you ask someone "How do you **feel** about …?" they will most certainly express their attitude, feeling or emotion about the topic. Note also that the first question started with 'What' and the second with 'How' which helped reinforce the fact or feeling response required.

To illustrate: Some years ago I was asked to do some personal coaching with John, the General Manager of a heavy-duty manufacturing plant. Although the plant was successful and profitable, John's CEO was concerned about the high turnover rate amongst John's senior management team. My first task was to get to know John, find out more about his role and about his relationships at work. Following an initial discussion, I sat-in on one of his management team meetings and early on Monday morning went with him as he did a tour of the factory (which he did every Monday).

Listening to John talk with the supervisors and factory workers, and during a team meeting, I was impressed with the high regard in which John was held. So why was there such a high turnover in his

CHAPTER NINE | THE PROCESS OF A CONVERSATION

team? Things like role structure, role clarification, conflict and so on were all ruled out – it was a well-run establishment – John was a very efficient manager. The thing that struck me was that every discussion was about fact and logic. There was a total absence of discussion or mention of feelings, emotions and attitudes. As a result there didn't seem to be much fun in the workplace.

During my subsequent discussion with John, I asked him to do one thing for me when he did his next rounds of the factory. "John, when you talk with each person next Monday, I'd like you to replace the word 'think' with 'feel'. So for example, when you are asking about progress on the ABC project, say 'How do you **feel** about the progress we're making?' rather than 'What do you **think** progress looks like on the ABC Project?'"

At my next session with John after his Monday 'feeling' exercise, he had one word to say – "Wow!" He then went on to explain that he had learnt so much more in his rounds this Monday than ever before. People were still talking about some of the factual stuff, but now they were also expressing how they felt about things. This was the missing link in John's work place – emotion. People need to know how others (and particularly their boss) are feeling about things. They also want to feel that there is a safe place where they can express their emotions, both positive and negative. And it's the same in every good relationship – both people want to know they can express their feelings openly and honestly and get a 'sympathetic ear' when they need one.

In a difficult and emotionally charged conversation, many people are not really listening to what others say. Instead, they are often mentally 'reloading' their responses. This means they may fail to pick up important clues about the other's emotions and concerns, which also means missing opportunities to build trust and understanding. The most common mistake we all make at one time or another is that

PART TWO | WORDS TO USE, WORDS TO AVOID AND OTHER INFLUENCING FACTORS WHEN COMMUNICATING

when emotions are running high, we tend to start speaking before the other person has finished (the 0.05 seconds overlap becomes far greater when emotions are high).

Listen, really listen. Listen with the 'third ear' (the one that picks up the unspoken meaning or feeling – this is quite often your intuition or gut feeling), both to what is being said and to what is not being said. It is important to note that you do not have to agree, but you do have to understand. The other person also needs to know that you understand. We often assume they know we understand but if we don't actually *tell* them that can be a dangerous assumption to make.

3. Construct Meaning: People are able to understand one another through previous conversations, shared knowledge, common language or social norms. This is achieved through skilled questioning which also enables you to bring to the surface and address people's underlying issues, needs and concerns. Questioning allows you to check assumptions – yours and theirs.

Be sure to ask lots of questions, both open and closed (e.g. who, what, when, how). The most powerful questions stimulate the other person to think differently.

Keep questions short. Ask one at a time (avoid compound questions) and pause for the reply. Use "Why?" sparingly, since "Why?" often evokes rationalisation and justification rather than reflection. Instead you could ask:

- How might we work together to resolve this difficulty? (remembering to follow the rule about 'We' mentioned earlier)
- What else?
- Tell me more?
- What would need to happen for things to be different?

CHAPTER NINE | THE PROCESS OF A CONVERSATION

Two of the most powerful questions I've ever used are "What else?" and "Tell me more?" – both of which are in a way saying 'and' a little differently. People I've coached keep coming back to me with reports that their most powerful question has become "What else?"

Also remember to listen for metaphors as explained in Chapter 4. In a difficult conversation metaphors are most likely to illustrate the feeling behind what the other person is saying.

4. Converge on Agreement: People share some understanding of the topic even if minimal, or a desire to understand it if the conversation is to continue (although they may totally disagree on one another's reasons, logic, philosophy and so on). Once again, questioning and listening are the keys here.

As the two of you start to reach agreement on the issue or problem and potential answers start being discussed, there's another form of questioning called 'Constraints Questions' that can be useful. These help you get a clearer picture of what is happening and what can be done to improve the situation:

- What stops you ...?
- What gets in the way ...?
- Do you have an example of ...?

And if you feel there is a need to look for further options, another useful tool is 'Hypothetical Questions'. For example:

- What if ...?
- If we could ...?
- If it were possible to do this, what would it look like?

These questions, together with effective listening (such as appropriate paraphrasing or preferably, Clean Language) are at the heart of reaching agreement.

Once you've completed Tasks 1 to 4:
1 – Open a Channel
2 – Commit to Engage
3 – Construct Meaning, and
4 – Converge on Agreement

then Task 5 – Evolve, and 6 – Act or Transact, should fall into place automatically.

5. Evolve: Either or both people are different after the conversation – this may be in their actions, beliefs or even a strengthening of their initial thoughts and ideas.

- What did the conversation identify, confirm or change for each person?
- How did each person feel following the conversation? Was this a different feeling from before?

6. Act or Transact: Either or both people do something as a result of the conversation – this may range from undertaking some action, telling someone else, or continuing to think (consciously) about the topic.

- What has each person done since the conversation (that was related)?
- Who have they told (or will they tell/involve) about the conversation? Why?

If it's important for you to know what the other person is going to do following the conversation, you could ask the following questions (depending on your circumstances):

- "Who are you going to tell about our discussion?"
- "What are you going to tell them?"
- "What will you do if they disagree with what we've decided?" OR "What should we do if others disagree with our decision?"

CHAPTER NINE | **THE PROCESS OF A CONVERSATION**

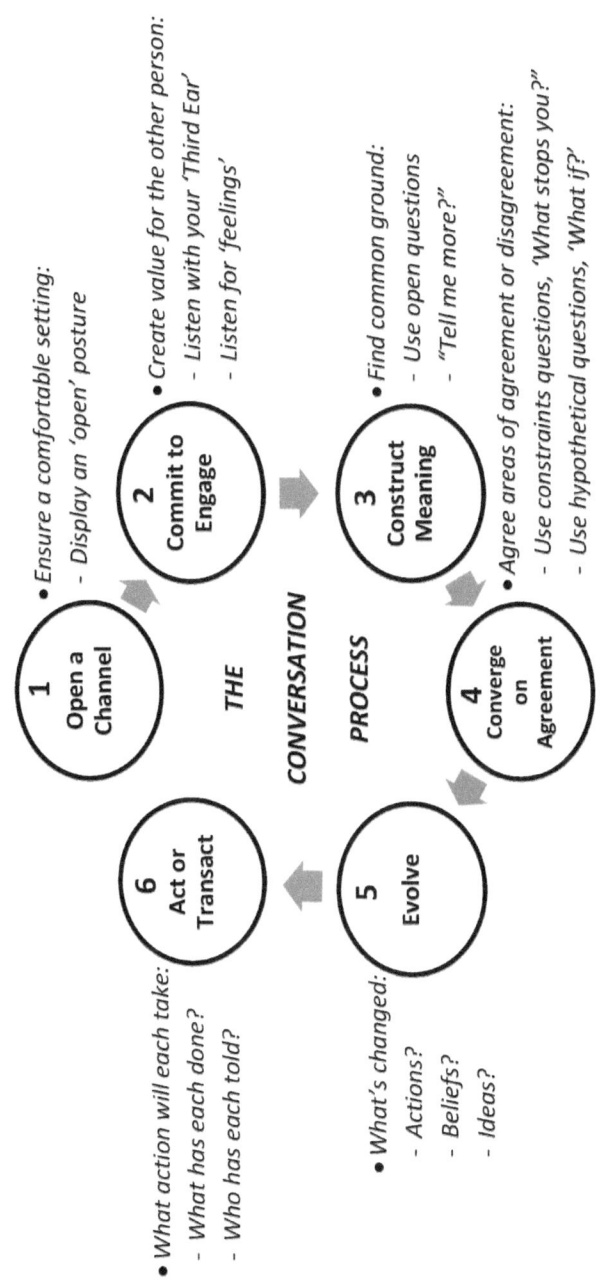

Earlier in this Chapter I said that it would be "nigh on impossible to remember all six of these tasks during a difficult or challenging conversation". As you've seen it really is only the first four you need to remember and manage during the conversation, so hopefully this Conversation Process will assist.

In the next part of this book I'll cover some of the challenging conversations many of us face. In a number of these I'll be explicitly outlining how the six tasks in the Communication Process are managed. In others it will be implicit – I'll leave it to you to discern when they are occurring.

Suggestions for practising Conversation Process Management

Managing the conversation process is a challenging skill to develop – it requires an understanding of the concept, a willingness to try it out, and practice and perseverance to develop competence. It's unlike some of the other concepts I've covered such as eliminating 'don't' which only requires practice. At this stage you may decide that knowledge of the concept is sufficient. However, if you really want to become effective at managing difficult conversations, I'd recommend trying one or both of exercises 1 and 2 in order to start developing this skill.

Exercise 1: How to become familiar with the Conversation Process

1. Briefly review the Process Management chart above. Make sure you're familiar with the meaning of each heading (particularly Tasks 1 to 4).

CHAPTER NINE | THE PROCESS OF A CONVERSATION

2. Observe: Within the next two or three days, as you participate in a conversation with two or more other people, try to identify what is happening to complete each of Tasks 1 to 4. (Although you are participating, being able to observe what the other two people are saying or not saying and doing should give you some real insights into how the conversation process is being managed and the tasks are being completed.)
3. As soon as possible after this conversation, take some time to jot down some answers to the following questions:

   1. Open a Channel:
   - Did the physical setting have any impact on how comfortable people felt about starting the conversation?
   - Was there anything you noticed about the participants' mannerisms that helped start the conversation?

   2. Commit to Engage:
   - What value do you think the people saw in the conversation? Why did they continue the conversation?
   - Why did the conversation end? Was this too soon, too long or about right?

   3. Construct Meaning:
   - What did the people share or have in common?
   - How did they discover this shared meaning?
   - Were there specific questions that people asked that facilitated a shared understanding?
   - What were some of the better questions you heard?

4. **Converge on agreement**
   - What did the participants agree on, or perhaps 'agree to disagree' on? Why?
   - How did they reach this agreement?

5. **Evolve**
   - What do you believe the conversation identified, confirmed or changed for each person?
   - How do you think each person felt following the conversation? Do you think this was different from how they felt before?
   - How did you feel before and after the conversation?

6. **Act or Transact**
   - What has each person done since the conversation (that was related and that you know of)?
   - Who have they told (or will they tell/involve) about the conversation? Why?

Exercise 2: An alternative, challenging exercise on conversation process management

If you'd like an exercise that's a little more challenging, try the following:

1. Invite (or coax, cajole, persuade or maybe even bribe) a good friend or trusted colleague to help you with this exercise (Note: The word 'trusted' is important here.)
2. Give him/her a copy of this Chapter and ask that they observe you in an upcoming conversation. They are to look for how the process of the conversation was managed by you. It can be useful if they have a copy of the Conversation Process Map as a guide.

CHAPTER NINE | **THE PROCESS OF A CONVERSATION**

3. Immediately following the conversation, ask them to answer the questions (under each task) as outlined in Exercise 1.
4. Find a quiet place; sit down and get their feedback.

Exercise 3: A less demanding exercise on conversation process management

1. When next you have completed a difficult conversation (where either you or the other person was the subject):
   - Take a few moments (once your emotional levels have subsided) to answer the questions outlined in Exercise 1.

Exercise 4: How to distinguish 'facts' and 'feelings' (this exercise ranges over three days)

1. Select two days where you are going to consciously identify when you use the words 'think' or 'feel' in questions throughout each day. It's a good idea to select 'think' on one day then 'feel' the following day (or vice versa).
2. At the end of each of days 1 and 2, reflect on your various conversations:
   - Do you know whether you used more 'think' or 'feel' questions?
   - What did you learn?
   - What did you hear more of from others?
   - How might this change the way you ask questions?
3. Decide that on the third day you will practise using your least preferred 'think' or 'feel' questions.
4. Alternatively, to gain a more objective view of your style, ask a friend to observe you for a day and then give you the feedback.

5. Once you start to become confident with using both 'think' and 'feel' questions, develop a list of other fact and feeling words that can elicit similar responses. For example, for 'fact': try 'analyse', 'describe', 'define'; and for 'feel': try 'passion', 'passionate', 'enthusiastic' (see my initial conversation with Alice to gauge how these might work – then develop your own).

Exercise 5: How to use constraints and hypothetical questions

When faced with your next difficult or challenging conversation, particularly one where the other person has an issue or problem that needs to be solved, practise using the following:

Constraints:
- What stops you …?
- What gets in the way …?
- Do you have an example of …?

Hypothetical:
- What if …?
- If we could …?
- If it were possible to do this, what would it look like?

Final comment:

As Brian Clark points out in his article *50 Trigger Words and Phrases for Powerful Multimedia Content*, "The difference between the right word and the almost right word is determined by the level of emotional identification that word prompts. In other words, the right emotional trigger words take the same basic message to all new heights. Don't

CHAPTER NINE | THE PROCESS OF A CONVERSATION

settle for lightning bugs on a clear summer night when you could be shooting for the stars."

There are growing bodies of experience, research, philosophies, principles and practices that teach us about the power of conversations (where the right words are used) to create breakthroughs. Where conscious and constructive conversation happens, trust begins, cooperation starts and violence disappears.

PART TWO | **WORDS TO USE, WORDS TO AVOID AND OTHER INFLUENCING FACTORS WHEN COMMUNICATING**

Summary – Don't: How using the right words will change your life

Where are we now?

The 'don't' rule ... (Chapter 1)

Completely eliminate the word 'don't' from your vocabulary. Think of what you would like (or want) people to do, and say so.

Accentuate the Positive, Eliminate the Negative ... (Chapter 2)

Eliminate as many negative words from your conversation, emails, texts and other communication as possible. Replace them with the positive alternative.

Apply the 'Futureless Concept' ('I am') when planning or talking about future events ... (Chapter 3)

Express the future as if it's already happening. For example, express things you are going to do as "I am" rather than "I will", "I must" or "I want to".

Use metaphors, particularly in your written communication and 'and' in conversations ... (Chapter 4)

Develop metaphors to suit the situation. Use 'and' (with an appropriate pause) to uncover the true meaning or feeling behind what someone else is expressing when they use a metaphor.

PART TWO | WORDS TO USE, WORDS TO AVOID AND OTHER INFLUENCING FACTORS WHEN COMMUNICATING

When feeling down, change the descriptions of your negative feelings into words that are 'quirky' and more positive (to make you smile) ... (Chapter 5)

Better still, use metaphors that will enable you to lighten up the negativity you may feel in a challenging or difficult situation.

Use 'I' instead of 'you' to express an issue or concern or to provide advice; avoid 'but' and replace it with 'yes, and' ... (Chapter 7)

- The 'I', 'you', 'we' rules:
  1. "**I** have a problem/issue/concern. This is how **I** see things ..."
  2. "How do **YOU** see it?" or "How can **YOU** help?" (depending on the issue and situation)
  3. "What can **WE** do to work through this issue?"
- and the 'yes, and' technique:
  4. Replace 'but' and 'yes, but' with 'yes, and'.

Check your tone ... (Chapter 8)

Make sure your tone of voice matches the words you use and your feelings.

Learn to manage the 'process' of a conversation ... (Chapter 9)

1. Open a Channel – check your location, mood, posture
2. Commit to Engage – create value for the other person – listen for feelings
3. Construct Meaning – find common ground – ask questions – "tell me more ..."
4. Converge on Agreement – search for areas of agreement – ask constraints and hypotheticals
5. Evolve – What's changed – Actions? Beliefs? Ideas?
6. Act or Transact – What will happen next? Who will be told?

PART THREE
Difficult conversations and how to manage these

Introduction to Part 3

Chapters here are stand-alone – to be used as and when you may face a difficult situation. Before you tackle one of these there are three concepts that will be helpful to understand further – *Framing, Triangulation* and taking an *'I' perspective*. All of these have been either mentioned explicitly or alluded to earlier but now need further explanation as a lead-in to Part 3.

1. Framing (or, as it is sometimes referred to, 'reframing')

Basically framing is looking at one's perspective of an issue as if examining it through a lens, so reframing is to change that perspective; to 'look at it from another angle'. For example you may be able to reframe your's or another person's perspective by changing the words you use such as:

- expressing a *problem* as an *opportunity*
- expressing a *weakness* as a *strength*
- expressing an *impossibility* as a *distant possibility*
- expressing a *distant possibility* as a *near possibility*
- expressing *unkindness* as *lack of understanding*

Although not specifically mentioned, I've used *reframing* extensively in Parts 1 and 2. Changing 'don't' to the positive is one example; turning negative 'self-talk' such as "What if I try and fail" into "This is working for me" is another.

In many difficult conversations we are aiming to reframe another's perspective. So the words we choose are important for example:

- *"Yes, it does seem stupid (REFRAME) and it may also be stupid not to look again and see what else can be done"*
- *"It's not so much doing away with old ways as (REFRAME) building a new and exciting future"*
- *"We've shown we can argue well (REFRAME) m*aybe this means we can also agree well*"*
- *"You say it can't be done in time (REFRAME) what if we staged delivery or got in extra help? I'm sure we can produce an acceptable product in the timeframe"*

In fact framing is often used by us in day-to-day conversation as a metaphor to describe someone's attitude as their 'frame of mind'. Here's an example of how a negatively framed message can be changed into a positive one:

Negative framing:
"I never seem to build lasting relationships. My last 'best friend' who I really got along with well, hasn't contacted me for weeks."
Positive framing:
"While my last close-friendship didn't seem to last long, I've learned some valuable lessons. Over the last few weeks I've had the chance

PART THREE | DIFFICULT CONVERSATIONS AND HOW TO MANAGE THESE

to really think hard about how I relate to people. I now realise that I have to be more open with people close to me if the relationship is going to blossom."

As Henry Ford is reported to have said, "If you think you can do a thing or you think you can't do a thing, either way you're right" – it's the words you use to frame it that propel you into action. As well as reframing your own words one of the main objectives in each of the difficult conversations covered in Part 3 is to influence others to reframe how they see things – to 'change their terms of reference'. Always keep in mind that their frame is valid (to them) and so it's important to start your conversation from that perspective, rather than saying "you're wrong" or merely thinking "they're wrong".

And reframing has another benefit – it can help you manage your emotions and when used successfully with others, can also help manage their emotional level. Psychologist James J. Gross has found that reframing (his term is 'cognitive reappraisal') when someone is emotionally aroused can lower their emotional level. For example, you may find yourself very angry that your partner forgot to buy the fish you had planned for dinner. You can lower your anger level by reframing such as "Fish is good, but there's a nice piece of chicken in the freezer that should be eaten as it will deteriorate if left there too long".

The key to effective reframing is to focus on the action that you intend to take or the behaviour you intend to change (i.e. 'fish' and 'chicken') not the feeling, 'anger'. That's the key – focus on behaviour rather than feelings. The trick is timing – to lessen the emotional impact of say a negative experience, you need to reframe straight away. If not, the brain goes into action to alert various sensing parts of the body that there is something wrong and so your heart rate increases, your face may turn red, you sweat, tremble or whatever else your body has learned to do when aroused. As the saying goes, "timing is everything".

PART THREE | DIFFICULT CONVERSATIONS AND HOW TO MANAGE THESE

Many Chapters in Part 3 will provide some suggestions as to how you can reframe your outlook and influence others to reframe their perspective in various challenging situations. In others I'll leave it to you to think about how you could reframe in this situation – it's a great skill to learn.

2. Triangulation

In geometry, "triangulation is the process of determining the location of a point by measuring angles to it from known points at either end of a fixed baseline, rather than measuring distances to the point directly". And in the social sciences, triangulation is often used to indicate that two (or more) methods are used in a study in order to check the results. So here I'm going to borrow from both disciplines to present a strategy that can be very useful in difficult conversations.

One of the challenges (that can be equally problematic or advantageous) in a difficult conversation is that the two people are standing facing one another. In a heated discussion this can be the 'stand up and fight' stance or perhaps the advice given to one as "You need to stand up to him". So we are often in fight, not flight mode when having a difficult conversation.

I've mentioned previously the need to 'open a channel' at the start of a conversation with such things as the words you use, your body language, where you have the conversation and the setting (e.g. comfortable chairs and even refreshments to make it easier for both people to have a productive dialogue). Triangulation is a further technique that can ease the situation when the conversation gets particularly challenging or even heated – it creates a feeling of partnership rather than competition. Triangulation can in fact re-open a channel that may have started to close up.

How do you triangulate?

PART THREE | DIFFICULT CONVERSATIONS AND HOW TO MANAGE THESE

For example in a tense business negotiation where two people seem to be at an impasse, it can be useful for one to say, "Let's look at what we've each put forward and see if we can appreciate each perspective from a different angle". Notice the words here "look at", "see", "each perspective", "different angle" – they are all visual and invite each person to examine the situation through a different lens. This new lens is also likely to be more optimistic (in finding a solution) because the positive word "appreciate" was used as part of the invitation (another example of 'priming').

One person then steps up to a whiteboard or flip chart and asks the other to summarise both proposals (or points of difference). The situation although not resolved, is now moving through to reaching an agreement on what has been covered. Up to this point there has been total disagreement; now for the first time they are working together – one writing, the other providing the information. The person recording may then invite the other to stand and take the pen and as they discuss each point, write a comment about how that could work (given certain circumstances). Both people although still standing, are now looking at the board not at each other – the issue or problem has been triangulated.

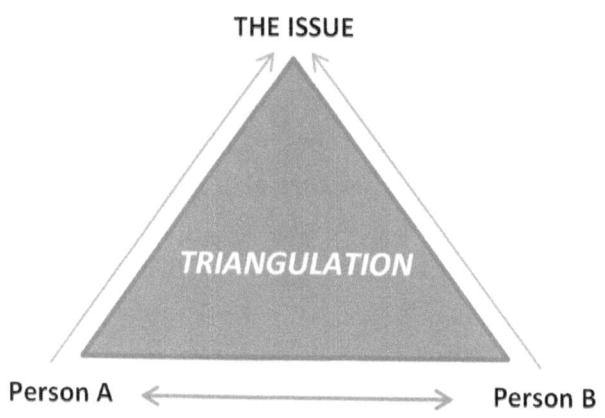

PART THREE | **DIFFICULT CONVERSATIONS AND HOW TO MANAGE THESE**

Similarly in a discussion between, say, parent and teenager, one could suggest that each write a few points down on a sheet of paper. The problem has now been triangulated so that both people focus on what's being written on the paper, not directly at one another.

Triangulation can even be done when there are no physical things to help such as paper or whiteboard, by using your hands. In this case the speaker looks down at both hands (held out in front of him/her), then while still looking down at his/her hands, moves both out to one side saying "Let's look at this from another perspective". It's quite fascinating to watch the other person now change their gaze from looking directly at the speaker to look at the speaker's hands and start to suggest some alternatives. Triangulation has occurred.

We'll see some other examples of triangulation in the Chapters to follow.

3. Taking an 'I' perspective

We've covered the technique of using 'I' messages in Chapter 7. As it's such an integral component of having a successful conversation it's also important to discuss the philosophy behind taking an 'I perspective.'

At first glance it may seem that using 'I' is just another seed in the burgeoning 'me' society that has mushroomed over the last couple of decades. This 'me' society or as it goes by its pseudonym *'i'* seems to be all pervasive – for example the *'i* phone', *'i* pad', *'i* net' and so on – the focus on the individual. All the marketing gurus have jumped on the band wagon (once Apple lost their court case to copyright *'i'*), so that now if a new product does not have a designation starting with *'i'* or as I've seen recently a double *'ii'*, it's not worth promoting.

However, taking an 'I' perspective in conversations is not about 'me' it's about taking responsibility for our words and actions. Although

PART THREE | DIFFICULT CONVERSATIONS AND HOW TO MANAGE THESE

described as a technique, it is both a conversational technique and a philosophy of approach. And there's also a sound scientific reason for taking an 'I' perspective. Studies have shown that taking an 'I' perspective can lead to:
- Greater valuing of others
- Greater helping of others
- A reduction in stereotyping of others and the groups to which they belong

In fact these studies also found that taking an 'I' perspective can lead to some overlap in self-concept between yourself and the other person, which means that when using 'I' the other person has an inclination to actually identify with you and you with them (as opposed to using 'you' which can lead to a widening of the gap between you). So viscerally it is a very powerful tool.

Using the Chapters in Part Three

If you've completed some of the exercises in Parts 1 and 2, then you can now apply the techniques learned to the difficult conversations covered in Part 3. If not, you may wish to revisit some as they come up in a particular conversational topic. Either way I trust that you find the suggestions here useful to some of the situations you face or may encounter.

CHAPTER 10

Spouse to spouse, or partner to partner

"We need to talk"

"We need to talk" (mental response from partner: *"Oh, Oh – I wonder what I've done?"*)

We often think of difficult or challenging conversations as inevitable, even in a caring, loving relationship. And they are. That doesn't mean they have to have poor outcomes. When emotions are high, and they generally will be in these situations because the stakes (the relationship) are also high, we often stumble over the words we use. In this Chapter I'll outline some of the words that can help make the conversation constructive and recap (as was seen in Parts 1 and 2) on some of the words to avoid that are likely to lead to a destructive, or at best, less than ideal outcome.

Before that I'm going to ask you a challenging question. What type of communicator are you when it comes to difficult conversations? To learn anything from this Chapter you'll need to be brutally honest with yourself (I'll disclose my natural style after you've read the following descriptions).

Communication experts generally agree that in spouse to spouse or partner to partner conversations where there are

CHAPTER TEN | SPOUSE TO SPOUSE, OR PARTNER TO PARTNER

difficult conversations occurring, there are four types of communicators:

1. Passive – this person tends to clam up when faced with a difficult situation, or they'll try and avoid the discussion. For example when finances are tight they will avoid discussing the issue even though they may see a disaster coming. They may try and fix it without having the conversation, which of course can lead to frustration and perhaps anger when their partner finds out. Passive communicators will try to hide their emotions which can lead to stress, resentment and bitterness – thinking "Why doesn't she do something about it? Can't she see there's a problem?"

2. Aggressive – as the title suggests, this type of communicator tends to be loud and tries to control. They can also attack and provoke the other with the words they use. They will often blame their partner or others such as family members for the problem. For example if there is a financial problem you could hear "You really need to watch the finances. Buying that new dress was a stupid thing to do when you know how tight our finances are".

3. Passive/Aggressive – these communicators tend to express their feelings in an indirect manner. At first they seem pleasant and warm, giving compliments which can however, be taken two ways but may actually be cheap jibes. They will deal with the problem by making hints or subtle suggestions while acting as if nothing is wrong. They are likely to make somewhat snarky comments about purchases or payments – "I'll bet that new dress was on special".

4. Assertive – this spouse starts with a very clear understanding of how they feel about the problem, what they think has led to it, and some ideas on how it could be fixed. They deal directly and honestly with the problem and have the conversation as soon as possible. While they are very clear about their feelings (and will express these) they are also very willing to listen to their partner once the problem has been clearly defined. With our finances example they will state the responsibility they have in causing the problem and be prepared to work together to solve it – "Hey, Darling, I'm feeling frustrated about our finances. It's not a big deal, but I need to talk about it and I need to hear from you".

From the descriptions it's obvious that the first three are somewhat negative and the fourth is more positive. Perhaps you may not see them as clear-cut as this and in your own case you can see a bit of yourself in more than one style. This is where I put up my hand. My natural style is 'passive' and I've been working for some time on developing a far more assertive (and in the process) open and honest style when faced with a difficult spouse conversation. For a 'passive' I have to admit that it's hard!

What's your natural style?

If you are aware of this and it's one of the first three – passive, passive/aggressive or aggressive, then the first step in managing a difficult conversation with your spouse or partner is to look at ways that you can moderate your natural style. And the best way of doing this is to be more assertive with the words you use. The following suggestions will help.

Note: before continuing it's important to understand what 'assertive behaviour' means. In common usage the word 'assertive' may seem negative and is often confused with 'aggressive' (e.g. the misconception that assertive people always get their way). However, assertiveness is the quality of being self-assured and confident without being aggressive. Assertive people tend to:

CHAPTER TEN | SPOUSE TO SPOUSE, OR PARTNER TO PARTNER

- feel free to express their feelings, thoughts and desires
- be able to initiate and maintain comfortable relationships
- have control over their anger
- be willing to compromise with others rather than (might be thought) always wanting their own way
- have high self-esteem

(If you need more information on assertiveness, Chapter 15 'The conversation you're having when you're not having a conversation' covers this in detail.)

Drs. John and Julie Gottman of the Gottman Institute suggest there are three steps to managing conflict in successful marriages. Having looked at over 3,000 marriage situations, they found that couples who are successful (who are happy, have a great relationship and stay together) all follow a three step process when bringing up a difficult situation with their partner (I'm sure you'll notice these strategies are the same as those which follow the Conversation Process discussed in Part 2 of the book and the techniques outlined earlier).

They start from an 'I' perspective where they immediately explain their feelings: 'I'm frustrated', 'I'm upset' or 'I'm angry'. This explanation of feelings is very important as it shows the depth of their emotion which could range for example from merely 'frustrated' to 'angry' and gives their partner a clear idea of the seriousness of the issue.

Secondly they explain the facts of the situation, not their perception – these are definite facts: for example "I'm upset that the garbage has not been put out regularly", or "I'm angry that there's a new dent in the car", or "I'm frustrated that the bills are not being paid on time". All of these are facts and are indisputable.

Finally they ask for help. For example, "What can you do to help me get the garbage out sooner?", "What can you do to help keep our car in good condition?", "How can you help me with getting the bills paid on time?"

The 4 Steps to managing a difficult conversation with your spouse or partner

To the three steps outlined by the Gottmans I've added an opening statement to start with, such as "Darling, I have a problem that I need your help with". So an example of the steps now becomes:

1. *"Darling, I have a problem that I need your help with"* – this is a call for help which **Opens a Channel** for the conversation to begin.
2. *"I'm frustrated"* – an expression of feeling which will **Commit the other person to Engage** – and they are likely to respond, *"Why are you frustrated Dear?"* or perhaps even a simple *"Oh?"* or maybe *"Really?"*.
3. *"I'm frustrated that the bills are not being paid on time"* – this states the facts that have led to the feeling and **Constructs the Meaning** for the conversation.
4. *"How can you help me with getting the bills paid on time?"* – this specifies the type of help needed and will also start the process to **Converge on Agreement**.

These four can be rolled into one statement:

"Hey, Darling, I have a problem that I need your help with. I'm feeling frustrated about our finances and in particular, the bills not being paid on time. It's not a big deal, but I need to talk about it and I need to hear from you. I'd really like your help. How can you help me with getting the bills paid on time?"

CHAPTER TEN | SPOUSE TO SPOUSE, OR PARTNER TO PARTNER

These four steps may be summarised as:

1. **Ask for help**
2. **Express your feelings**
3. **Say why you are feeling this way**
4. **Ask for specific ways or type of help needed**

Although assertive, "In really good relationships, people are very gentle with the way they talk about a potential conflict," John Gottman says. "They don't bare their fangs and leap in there; they're very considered." You can readily see that our example conversation above will lead very quickly to a joint discussion of the problem – both partners will now work together to solve the issue in a rational, not emotional manner.

Please read over the example again as it follows the four steps:

The 4 steps:	Statement:	Why the 4 steps to start managing the conflict situation work:
1. Ask for help	"Darling, I have a problem that I need your help with"	Opens the channel
2. Express feelings	"I'm frustrated"	This feeling provokes interest in the other person *to engage* in the conversation
3. Say why you are feeling this way	"I'm frustrated that the bills are not being paid on time"	*Constructs meaning* around the topic so that the other person understands why this feeling
4. Ask for the specific help needed	"How can you help me with getting the bills paid on time?"	'Request for help' commences the process where the two people can *converge on agreement*

PART THREE | DIFFICULT CONVERSATIONS AND HOW TO MANAGE THESE

The rationale behind these four steps is:
- The speaker is working from an 'I' perspective. There is neither blame nor criticism.
- He is taking and showing his responsibility for the situation.
- He is asking for help – to which probably 99% of the population will always respond positively.
- By verbalising his feeling of frustration, he is automatically lowering his emotional level.
- He's only using 'you' in the future tense when asking for help. So, it now becomes a joint problem to solve.

Note that it's not prudent nor realistic to try to script your difficult conversation from start to finish. After all, your partner has not seen the script! In fact if you try it will most likely be seen at best as fake and at worst as insincere – you could be worse off than before you started.

Although you can't script the conversation you can do three things:
1. *Practise your opening statements* (as suggested above). Getting these right will start the conversation off on a sound footing.
2. Keep in mind that you need to *open the dialogue*, get your partner *committed to engaging* in the conversation, make sure you *both understand the meaning* (facts) of the situation and *work towards agreement*. To achieve these aims you will need to ask plenty of questions (remember the 'and ...' technique) and listen carefully for the underlying emotions.
3. *Remain calm and centred*. The best way of doing this is to avoid 'you' (only use it in the future tense), 'but' and 'yes, but' – if you actively think about following these rules as you have your conversation you will remain calm (your logical brain has been engaged).

CHAPTER TEN | **SPOUSE TO SPOUSE, OR PARTNER TO PARTNER**

What to do when your partner starts the conversation

So that's one side of the story. But what happens when your partner hits you with a topic, issue or problem which they seem quite emotional about, and one that is also likely to raise your emotional levels? What do you do? How do you respond?

Saying things like "Calm down", "Cool it", "Chill out" or perhaps "Don't get so emotional" (not that any of us are likely to use that last one after learning about the 'don't' rule) are not effective. In fact labelling the emotion of the other person often raises their emotional level. Why is this? Apparently we're not very good at recognising our own emotions in a stressful situation. Then when someone else presumes to tell us that we are in any way emotional (such as "Don't get so emotional"), we take affront. So what do you do?

Dr. Albert J. Bernstein, a clinical psychologist, has three magic tricks that he suggests you use:

1. "Please speak more slowly. I'd like to help"
2. "What would you like me to do?"
3. Ask questions – any questions will do, but the best are questions to clarify

Can you see the rationale behind these three 'tricks'?

In trick 1 "Please speak more slowly. I'd like to help" two things are happening. Firstly instead of responding emotionally (as your partner might expect), you respond rationally with a request. This throws the other person off their game for the moment. They have to stop and mentally ask themselves "Am I speaking too quickly?" Posing such a rational question triggers the 'little voice in their head' which immediately starts their rational brain working. In the process this

PART THREE | DIFFICULT CONVERSATIONS AND HOW TO MANAGE THESE

begins to lower their emotional level. Surprisingly this works even if they are already speaking quite slowly.

Secondly, you are offering help. This is generally totally unexpected by the other person so soon into the conversation. It shows that you are prepared to listen and also prepared to work towards a solution.

In trick 2 "What would you like me to do?" you are throwing the responsibility for outlining the problem, and most importantly, making some suggestions as to how it might be resolved, back onto your partner. Once again this engages their rational brain to do a fair bit of explaining and importantly, to start talking about the future rather than the past. Their emotional barometer drops another notch. (Be careful with your tone of voice here – make sure this is a genuine question.)

By the time you get to trick 3 you will have heard a lot about the problem and why it is a problem to your partner. Their emotional level should also have dropped a few more notches. This is where it's very important to pull out of your top-hat Bernstein's third magic trick – 'ask questions'.

It's very tempting at this point to put your side of the story – particularly if you have some disagreement with something they've said or their rationale. Hold sway! Now's the time to 'get into their world' by using a number of questions. You'll have gathered some hints from the conversation as to which questions to ask – any will do, although questions to clarify are the most useful and make sure they are open – try to avoid 'Why?' type questions as they can lead to criticism and blame. If you cannot think of a question, remember from our earlier discussions the following general questions will stand you in good stead and move the conversation productively forward:

- What else?
- Tell me more?

CHAPTER TEN | **SPOUSE TO SPOUSE, OR PARTNER TO PARTNER**

- How might we work together to resolve this difficulty? (Remember – always follow the rule about 'I', 'you', 'we')
- What would need to happen for things to be different?

The three tricks for rationalising a difficult situation that your partner raises are:

1. "Please speak more slowly. I'd like to help"
2. "What would you like me to do?"
3. Ask questions – any questions will do, but the best are questions to clarify

Final comments:

If you intend to bring up something with your partner that you believe will be difficult to discuss, you need to have the right energy levels. If you're coming from a place of frustration – it will not be a constructive conversation. To prepare you need to think, "What's the best way for this person to hear the message?" Then prepare the words you will use to initiate the conversation by following the four-step process outlined earlier.

And if you get hit with an unexpected outburst from your partner, then it's almost certain that this is a very stressful situation for them. Stressful conversations differ from other conversations because of the emotional loads they carry. These conversations call up embarrassment, confusion, anxiety, anger, pain or fear – if not in us, then in our spouse or partner. It's times like this that you need to put your magic cape and top-hat on and perform those three magic tricks.

There are no suggested exercises for this Chapter – I think they would be pointless. Instead I recommend that you re-read this Chapter

PART THREE | DIFFICULT CONVERSATIONS AND HOW TO MANAGE THESE

and consign to memory the **4 Steps for initiating a conversation** that may be difficult with your partner, and the **3 Magic tricks** for managing their emotional outbursts. Then when one or the other situation does come along you'll be well prepared.

Above all when arranging to talk with your spouse or partner please avoid the phrase "We need to talk" – these four words could not only kill off any chance of a meaningful, positive conversation, they may just trigger the start of the end of the relationship.

CHAPTER 11

Parent conversation with a young adult

How can you engage, really engage, with your son or daughter?

"Why do I have to get stuck with such dumb parents?"
And you know what? They're right!

It's not that we parents are 'dumb' it just seems that way to some teenagers. Why? During the teenage years people are very black and white in their thinking – there are no shades of grey as can be seen by older adults. In fact people do not mature emotionally until their mid-twenties. The limitations of the teenage brain have been well publicised in the mass media. This media attention and coverage is helping parents, teachers and others understand why it may be difficult for our teenage children to meet our expectations for managing emotions, handling risks, responding to relationships and engaging in complex school work or employment. For instance we now know that much of the difficulty in conversing with teenagers is due to the fact that in early and mid-adolescence their brain undergoes considerable growth and pruning, moving generally from back to front areas of the cerebral cortex. Hence we can see wild swings in both reason and emotion over short periods of time.

PART THREE | **DIFFICULT CONVERSATIONS AND HOW TO MANAGE THESE**

At the same time as young adults are learning and experiencing new things about the world, the very parts of the brain that process things such as impulses and emotions, calibration of risk and reward, problem-solving, prioritising, thinking ahead, self-evaluation and long-term planning are changing rapidly.

As a parent how do you manage in such changing times?

"Dad, I can see your logic, but I don't agree with you".

This is a huge topic, so in this Chapter I'll focus specifically on the difficult conversations you may have to have with these 'learning brains' and how to manage these productively. I'll leave it to others to explore the myriad relationship and other complex issues of parenthood.

How do I have 'the' conversation with my 'learning' teenager?

Remember our process of managing difficult conversations – open (a channel), engage, construct meaning, converge on agreement, evolve and act or transact – these are all particularly relevant in these discussions with your teenager.

How do I open?

When considering your approach, take into account the factors that are relevant or important to teenagers in general:
- They are in a learning phase.
- Their logic is superb. However, the potential for misunderstanding is high – they see things in black and white whereas in reality (and for us) it is often grey.

CHAPTER ELEVEN | PARENT CONVERSATION WITH A YOUNG ADULT

- They are 'embarrassment averse' – being embarrassed particularly in front of their friends, or even siblings, is almost terminal.
- They like being approached as an adult. They do not like being lectured to. They need to be listened to and heard.
- They have a high sensitivity to double standards and dishonesty – if you are being dishonest they will pick up on it very quickly and dismiss anything you are saying. For example if discussing drugs and you drink alcohol regularly, they are likely to dismiss your argument against drug use.
- They are hyper sensitive to criticism.
- And finally, they know much more than parents think. For example particularly the discussions they have with their peers around sex.

Your son or daughter may also be developing a real sense of dedication or commitment to a topic, cause or value at this time, so for example 'integrity', 'friendship', 'loyalty' or perhaps 'climate change', 'equality' or other social issues could be a key driver for them. Consider the value or issue that is foremost for your son and/or daughter so that you can build this into the conversation at the appropriate time, for example:

"John, I know that personal integrity is really important to you. I can see that. So in this instance ..."

Remember also that it's important to do some self-reflection and be aware of how you normally behave with your children:

- *Am I a controlling parent?* e.g. How often do you use questions such as "Do you understand?", to which the only response can

be a "Yes" (no matter what they are thinking). Such questions only reinforce the parent/child authority status.
- *Do I listen to my teenager (really listen)?* e.g. If I were to record a discussion between you and your son/daughter, what percentage of time would I hear you listening – 20%, 40%, 80%? It's estimated that when people are listening effectively, they are quiet for 80% of the conversation.
- *Do I allow my teenager's opinions and tastes to differ from my own?* e.g. How often do you watch, say, a YouTube clip (for teenagers) and ask your son or daughter for their opinion – and really listen to what they have to say without judgment? A recent study showed that 40% of teenagers who openly voiced their opinions to their parents at age 13 by age 15 and 16 were more likely to say "No" when pressured by peers to take drugs or alcohol.

Wow! I trust there's some honest self-examination going on here. If you're in any way kidding yourself about your answers to these questions your teenager will see right through it, lessening the effectiveness of the following suggestions.

So how do I open the conversation?

Before looking at the most appropriate words, it's essential to find the best time and place for the teenager discussion. For example over the dinner table is probably not the best place and time to discuss critical issues as it may heighten their embarrassment (unless of course this has become traditionally the place to discuss these openly in your household). Far better, particularly for a one-on-one, to talk with the teenager at the time that the two of you (or three if both parents

CHAPTER ELEVEN | **PARENT CONVERSATION WITH A YOUNG ADULT**

are involved) are doing something together that you all enjoy. This automatically gives you some common ground.

It can also be helpful if you have the conversation when travelling to the event in the car or even walking. Here you are automatically triangulating the conversation – you are side-by-side and the issue is out in front of you both. Triangulation for teenagers can be particularly important as it helps to overcome any embarrassment the face-to-face conversation may bring on.

Note: extremely important point. As you are no doubt aware, get them away from their screens. If they continue to text or fiddle with their phones, tablets etc., then you have very little chance of having a meaningful conversation.

How do I engage with my son or daughter?

My experience suggests that this is the most difficult aspect for parents. After all if it's a touchy subject such as sex or drugs, you've probably given it a good deal of thought and in the process perhaps become a little stressed (you probably also have the answers you think they should follow).

Framing is important here. Make sure it's all about learning and not blame. In fact try and use the word 'learn' as much as possible as this is what they are doing. For example,

> *"This may be something you will want to learn. I had to learn it as well."*

This also fits well with their frame of reference as they are in a constant state of learning – school, college, friends, relationships, and so on.

PART THREE | **DIFFICULT CONVERSATIONS AND HOW TO MANAGE THESE**

My suggestion is to use the standard conversation process. Remember you can only script the opening – the words and discussion will develop from there so make your start a good one:

1. **Open** the channel by asking for their help. For example;
   "John, I have an issue that I need your help with".
   You could change 'issue' to topic, subject, problem, concern, challenge etc., depending on the topic and the extent of emotion it is raising in you. Always keep it as a request for help.

2. **Engage** them by expressing the feeling that has led to your emotions being raised. For example:
   "I'm worried" or concerned/anxious/afraid/apprehensive – whatever your feelings are.
   Pause. This can be really tough – remain silent. Eventually they will respond (it may seem like an eternity, but is likely to be only seconds). *"What are you worried about Mum?"*

3. **Construct meaning** around the topic;
   "I'm worried that ...". This is where you construct meaning for them so that although these are your concerns, they should be expressed in a way that your daughter or son can relate to them.

4. **Converge on agreement** (this may take some time). A good starting request is;
   "How can you help me overcome my concern?"
   As the conversation progresses, keep in mind:
   - They are hyper sensitive to criticism. So a way of giving some constructive criticism might start with *"It's important for you to know ..."*
   - Work with their emotions – let them flow – sometimes you will need to ask questions. At other times saying nothing can

be appropriate and effective. As one parent reported recently his son said *"Dad, I don't want you to say anything. I'm angry and when you ask questions, I get less angry"*.
- They are trying on a role. They like being given responsibility. Look for examples where they can take some responsibility.
- Respect their perspective – which may shift quite rapidly during the conversation.
- You will need to control the pace of the conversation more so than between two adults. So your tone should be slower and more monotone than might normally be the case. This too will be a challenge as the conversation may be raising your emotional level. However, concentrating on the pace will also help reduce your emotional level.

5. Remember every **conversation evolves** so that both people are different as a result. You want this to be a positive experience for your young adult. How do you feel? How do they feel? One way of making an assessment is to ask them what they are going to say (to others) and do as a result of this discussion. This should be a genuine enquiry, not an inquisition to see if your message got through. For example, you could say;

   "John, I really find talks like these tough, but also very helpful. How do you feel? I'm also really interested to know what you think. What will you tell your friends about our talk?"

6. Finally **(act or transact)** because there is still an authority issue in the relationship. Ultimately you still have responsibility for their welfare; there must be an agreement as to how consequences for non-performance of their agreed responsibility will be handled.

For example, if the conversation has led to a change in their responsibilities, a good way of testing the impact it has had is to discuss 'consequences' (in a positive way). You could say:

"John, thanks for agreeing to take this on. I'm confident now that this will work. On the very slim chance that it doesn't, what's a fair consequence if you do not meet your responsibility?"

If they are too hard or too soft on themselves, then raise the issue of fairness;

"How's that fair on me/you?"

Addendum

In the next Chapter "Teenage conversation with parents – How can you talk about really difficult subjects with Mum and Dad?" I've suggested some ways teenagers might express their worries, embarrassment or concerns with you. So that you're prepared, following are three of the questions you might receive – how will you respond?

CHAPTER ELEVEN | PARENT CONVERSATION WITH A YOUNG ADULT

Teenager's question:	My response would be …	and then I will …
"Mum, I need to talk with you. I feel really *worried* that I may have let you down. Can I tell you what happened?"		
"Dad, I need to talk with you. It's kind of *embarrassing*. Is that OK?"		
"Mum, I have something to tell you. It's not the best news and I'm not proud of what I've done. I'm really *concerned* that you will be mad with me. But I know I need to tell you. Can you hear me out?"		

PART THREE | **DIFFICULT CONVERSATIONS AND HOW TO MANAGE THESE**

Final comment:

Remember it's a period of **challenge** for young adults as they frequently question parental authority. They can go to great lengths to remind you that you aren't the font of all wisdom as they once thought!

Will they ever get over having a 'dumb parent'?

CHAPTER 12

Teenage conversation with parents

How can you talk about really difficult subjects with Mum and Dad?

Did you know that 81% of parents feel comfortable talking about sex with their teenage children? A recent study also showed that only 50% of teenagers felt the same. So your parents are more likely to be comfortable when talking about difficult subjects such as sex and drugs than you may think. That should be a bit comforting to know.

And another study found that people at age 13 who were more open in expressing their opinions with their parents, by age 15 and 16 were far more likely to say "No" when pressured by their peers about drugs and alcohol (I've also repeated this finding in the Chapter for parents).

So there's some good evidence to suggest that the difficult conversation you need to have with your parents may not be as confronting for them as you may think and may also have some good spin-offs for you. But it can still seem difficult!

The aim of this Chapter therefore is to provide some tips that may help you with that difficult conversation you need to have with your parents. And although I'm not a teenager (though I once was, just like

PART THREE | **DIFFICULT CONVERSATIONS AND HOW TO MANAGE THESE**

your parents), I've called on the help of some teenagers to write this Chapter with me.

Kidshealth.org suggests a three step process to help make the difficult conversation with your parents flow more easily:
1. Know what you want from the conversation
2. Identify your feelings
3. Pick a good time to talk

1. Know what you want from the conversation

How would you like your parents to respond? For example:
- **Do you want them to just listen?**
  If so, this may be challenging as parents will invariably want to offer advice. You could say, "Mum, I want to tell you something. I'm not looking for your thoughts or ideas – I know you'll have some – I just want you to listen. Is that OK?" Notice here the words "I want to <u>tell</u> you something" not "I want to <u>talk</u> about something". The word 'tell' indicates a one-way street whereas 'talk' signals you want a discussion. Also the question "Is that OK?" asking for permission can be very useful – they can really only say "Yes" and that gets the conversation off to a good start.
- **Do you want them to support you or give you permission for something?**
  Start with your request for help or assistance – "Dad, I need your help. I would really love to go on the skiing excursion. I know it will be expensive. I need to know what I will have to do to be able to go. How can you help me?" In your request you are doing three things – asking for help, showing how you are willing to work towards the trip and then repeating your request for help.

CHAPTER TWELVE | TEENAGE CONVERSATION WITH PARENTS

- **Do you want to ask for their advice?**
  The first question to answer here is which parent to approach? You could go to both if you feel comfortable with a three-way conversation. However, often there will be subjects that you know you will be more comfortable discussing with one or the other. As one teenager said, "I know that I'd be more comfortable talking about sex with Mum than with Dad".

  If the subject is one that should (or you know will) be discussed by both parents and you decide to approach only one, then it's important to know what that parent will say to the other. "Dad, I know that you'll be talking with Mum about this, what are you going to tell her? It's a bit of a touchy subject for me, what words will you use to tell Mum?" Here your parent will start to think about the words he/she is going to use to tell the other. Phrase this question in your own words as you would say it – but make sure to use 'words' in your question as this is what you want to hear – their words.

- **Do you have to tell them something about a mistake you've made?**
  This can be one of the toughest conversations as you will most probably feel a bit guilty. For instance you may have broken something, broken a promise to them, done something wrong at school or perhaps felt that you've let them down in some way. The first thing to keep in mind is that everyone, yes everyone, has done something at some stage that they're not proud of – even your parents. "I'm not going to die or anything. I'm quite OK. But this isn't the greatest news" is how one teenager phoned her parents when she'd crashed her bike. Number one concern all parents have is their children's safety. In this example she has allayed that fear and

PART THREE | **DIFFICULT CONVERSATIONS AND HOW TO MANAGE THESE**

let the parents know that she was OK, but there was a non-threatening caveat – "this isn't the greatest news" – which was a nice lead into what she'd done.

Above all make sure you have the conversation face-to-face. Texting or emailing will kill off the potential of a successful outcome.

2. Identify your feelings

When the topic you want to discuss is sensitive or maybe embarrassing, it's important to identify how you feel about it and say so. For example:

- If you are **worried** that you may have let your parents down, you could say,

    "Mum, I need to talk with you. I feel really *worried* that I may have let you down. Can I tell you what happened?"

- If you feel **embarrassed** about something you've done or it's an embarrassing subject,

    "Dad, I need to talk with you. It's kind of *embarrassing*. Is that OK?"

- If you feel **concerned** that you've hurt someone,

    "Mum, I have something to tell you. It's not the best news and I'm not proud of what I've done. I'm really *concerned* that you will be mad with me. But I know I need to tell you. Can you hear me out?"

Notice in all these examples the person has:
1. Asked for help
2. Expressed his/her feelings
3. Concluded by asking permission to talk about it

CHAPTER TWELVE | TEENAGE CONVERSATION WITH PARENTS

3. Pick a good time to talk

Although most people are freshest in the morning, they are also rushing to prepare for the day. Evenings may be better, however, be aware of meal prep etc. Often the best times are when the two (or three) of you are doing something that you all enjoy. This gives you some common ground. Another good time is when you are walking together or travelling in the car (here you are triangulating the conversation as was mentioned in the Introduction to Part 3).

Make sure you ask about the timing:
- "Can we talk? Is now a good time?"
- "I need to talk with you. When would be a good time?"

Some tips that other teenagers suggest will help with that difficult conversation

- *Build trust through honesty:*
  "Build trust with your parents; this makes it easier when you have something difficult to tell them"
  "Avoid not telling things, keeping things hidden"
- *Overcome your parents' 'knowledge bank':*
  "Parents know more stuff. They have done more things. They have more experience. So be sure of your facts and find common ground – something both of you agree on"
- *Deal with parents' interrogation:*
  "Parents ask lots of questions. Have plenty of examples ready. Saying "I don't know" just pisses them off. If you really don't know the answer, say that you will find out or try to find out"
- *Defuse parents' anger:*
  "Mum, I can see that you're angry. I'm sorry that this is upsetting – it is for me too. What can I do to help?"

PART THREE | DIFFICULT CONVERSATIONS AND HOW TO MANAGE THESE

"When my Dad says 'I'm not angry, I'm just worried'. You can see that look in his eyes and you know he's angry. I would much rather deal with anger than worry. I can see that he's angry so why not say so?"

- *Overcome disagreements:*
  When you disagree and they say 'No, you're wrong', the worst thing to do is argue. Just ask loads of questions, find out where they're coming from. This shows that you're interested in what they've got to say and can lead to a better discussion, not an argument.
- *Talking about difficult or embarrassing things:*
  "The only way to deliver a difficult message without your emotions getting in the way is to rehearse it. Play it out in your head – "If they say …" then "I could say …"

Great advice! Here are some further tips I've discovered:
- *What happens when your parents spring something on you?* They want to talk about a difficult topic and you're not ready? You could suggest:
  "Dad, I need to think a bit more about this. It's obviously very important, so I want to be clear and not go off half-baked. Can we talk more about this tomorrow (evening/morning when you know that both of you have time)?" If they insist, you may need to be more assertive, "Dad, I know this is really important – it is to me too. That's why I really need time to think about it. Can I ask for the time to think about it?" (Also read the Chapter on 'Asserting' which provides some further tips and advice)
- *Find out what turns your parents on.* Do a bit of study or research about their favourite topic, sport or activity. Surprise your parents.

CHAPTER TWELVE | TEENAGE CONVERSATION WITH PARENTS

- *Try to understand their point of view.* There is no need to agree with your parents on everything, but you do need to understand where they're coming from. Telling your parents that you understand their views and feelings helps them to be willing to understand yours. "Mum, I understand what you're saying and I can see that it's really worrying you. Can I also explain how I see it and how I feel about it?" Notice that in this example, although you may disagree with what your parent is saying, you've not said so – you've accepted what she said (not agreed) and just asked permission to put your point. This approach will lead to a constructive discussion rather than an argument.

In summary, whatever the topic:
- Ask for their help
- Express your feelings
- Ask permission to talk about it

Some final comments:

Whether you are 6, 16 or 60 you're parents always have a feeling of responsibility about your welfare. Therefore whenever you approach them with a difficult subject, their first reaction is likely to be worry or concern. I trust this Chapter has given you some advice on how to allay their concerns and at the same time a few tips on how best to approach that difficult conversation.

Above all, prepare what you ae going to say. According to my sources, many teenagers practise what they are going to say to their parents. Sometimes they will even do this with a friend. Can I suggest that you take it one step further? Write out the words you are going to

PART THREE | **DIFFICULT CONVERSATIONS AND HOW TO MANAGE THESE**

start with then your difficult conversation will have a strong foundation to build on. Oh, and by the way, if you've not already read the Chapter on 'Parent conversation with a young adult' it may be a good idea to do so and find out how they are going to approach a difficult conversation with you – remember 'knowledge is power'.

CHAPTER 13

Conversation with an ageing parent

A heart-to-heart discussion

As our parents grow older we tend to see them as less active, both physically and mentally. However, while this may often be true of their physical prowess, their mental ability is frequently as sharp as it has ever been. This is particularly so if they have kept themselves mentally active and alert. As a result we may enter the discussion about their future labouring under a load of misapprehension.

The other aspect in our relationship that changes over time is 'dependency'. When we were younger, we depended on them for physical, moral, emotional and even perhaps monetary support. We've watched them make decisions for us, for them, for the family. Now the roles are starting to be reversed. Although they may evidence this change in roles it's sometimes hard for them to come to grips with it – this is particularly so if you see the need to change some of the major things in their life such as where they live, and they do not. They still want to be in control, and rightly so (assuming of course they are still mentally able to manage such decisions).

And then there's the adage that 'older people are set in their ways'. This is not strictly true. It's just that older people do like the familiar

PART THREE | **DIFFICULT CONVERSATIONS AND HOW TO MANAGE THESE**

(perhaps more so than younger people) and are quite adaptable to change, provided they choose to change. Therein lies the nub of the issue: 'choice'.

In fact it's been suggested that the subjective quality of life considerations for ageing seniors are:
- security,
- freedom,
- peace of mind,
- friends and
- choices.

So the conversation with your elderly parents could indeed be quite challenging. Before we get to the words to use and those to avoid, there are a couple of points to consider which may impact when, where and how you have that conversation:
- Is your relationship a 'drop by for coffee' one, or all business?
- Have you raised any similar issues in the past? If so, what was the result?
- Will it be just you having the conversation, or will you need to gain the support of other relatives, particularly siblings?
- How open are your parents to discussing such sensitive issues?

Your relationship with your parents – how open is it?

Chances are if yours is a 'drop by for coffee' relationship – which means you meet and talk regularly about all types of things – then it's likely that your parents will be quite open about a discussion on their future. If not then you will need to be far more careful and circumspect

CHAPTER THIRTEEN | **CONVERSATION WITH AN AGEING PARENT**

in the words you use, particularly those to open the discussion. For example openings that are NOT likely to work well with this type of parent are:
- "How's the house? It must be hard to keep this place in good shape."
- "How's your health? What's the doctor saying these days?"
- "How's the car? Still driving to the shops every weekend?"

Why will these not work? They sound pretty innocent. Two reasons; firstly while they all may look like questions they are in fact quasi statements of what you think about your parents' current abilities and situation. Secondly, as your parents will be aware, if you had a more engaging relationship you'd already know the answers – they may see these questions as an affront or below their dignity to respond.

How to plan for 'that' conversation

In planning the conversation there are two aspects to differentiate and be clear on:
1. The *need for* the conversation and how you will gain agreement from your parents to have it, and
2. The *actual conversation* about their future.

Sometimes these two will happen at the same time and in the same conversation. However, always keep in mind that you have two objectives; firstly to obtain agreement from your parents to have the discussion and secondly, to reach agreement on certain issues with your parents about their future. Often we neglect (to our detriment) the first objective and move straight to the options for their future – this invariably invites push back from our parents.

PART THREE | **DIFFICULT CONVERSATIONS AND HOW TO MANAGE THESE**

To be effective begin by asking yourself (and please be honest here):
- Why do you want to have this conversation?
- What do you want for yourself?
- What do you want for your parents?
- What are your fears or concerns?
- What would be your best-case scenario?
- What do you want to happen?
- What do you not want to happen?

Have you raised any similar issues in the past? If so, what were the results?

If you've raised similar issues in the past with mixed success, then your parents are likely to be defensive now. So once again the words to start the conversation should be well considered. For example the following can work well:

> "Last time I raised the topic of the future, I got the feeling that it was not well received. (Mum or Dad), I'm really concerned about your health. I really need to have this discussion with you so that together we can talk about the future."

Notice that this opening is discussing <u>the conversation</u>, not *options for their future:*
- "I raised the topic"
- "I got the feeling"
- "it was not well received"
- "I really need to have this discussion"
- "together we can talk about …"

CHAPTER THIRTEEN | CONVERSATION WITH AN AGEING PARENT

You'll recognise the 'I' perspective used to discuss the previous conversation and the speaker's need for a further discussion. Only once was health mentioned and that was to show the speaker's real concern and feeling. You will also notice that 'we' was used. This could be a small gamble as the parents have not agreed to have the discussion yet (or perhaps again). However, in this instance I believe it gives them a valid reason – 'the future' (not 'their future' which could be more intimidating words) as to why you want to have the discussion.

Who else should be involved in the discussion about your parents' future and the subsequent conversation with them?

If you're an only child then it will undoubtedly be you – perhaps also your partner or spouse, provided he/she has a good relationship with your parents and can add value to the conversation.

Keep in mind that every other person (including siblings) adds a further level of complexity to the conversation. This does increase the degree of difficulty in managing the conversation, particularly if it becomes more problematic. Various siblings may have different agendas.

So it's important to discuss the issue with your siblings and decide on a strategy for approaching and managing the conversation. Note: Your siblings will want to talk about the various options open to your parents. That's fine; but keep in mind that it's your parents' choice, not theirs (unless as was said earlier they are incapable of making these decisions). The purpose of the discussion with your siblings is to:

- Decide how best to approach the conversation with your parents

- Agree on what will be said to start the conversation
- Agree who will take which role during the conversation, for example:
  - Who will manage the conversation process, i.e. keep everything on track and manage the process?
  - Who will discuss various options?
  - Who will move the conversation forward to a conclusion?
- Agree what will not be said – this is equally as important as what will be said

It may also be useful to ask your siblings the same questions you pondered yourself – this way you'll know where they're coming from:
- Why do you want to have this conversation?
- What do you want for yourself?
- What do you want for your parents?
- What are your fears or concerns?
- What would be your best-case scenario?
- What do you want to happen?
- What do you not want to happen?

This may seem like overkill as I can hear some readers saying "surely we can just sit down and talk about it". In essence that's true. Keep in mind that this may be a big change for your parents and they have to make the final decision – trying to 'sell' them on one of your preferred options may prove very difficult (as an aside I'm amazed at the number of so called 'communication experts' who suggest selling strategies such as when talking about assisted-living facilities "call it a 'community' rather than a 'facility'" – such fake strategies never work).

To ensure all siblings are working harmoniously may I suggest that you give them a copy of this Chapter to read before you have the discussion?

CHAPTER THIRTEEN | **CONVERSATION WITH AN AGEING PARENT**

How do I start the conversation with my parents? How do I keep it on track?

- How to start the conversation:
  Open the Channel – *Request help*: "I (or 'We' if you are speaking on behalf of your siblings) have a subject that I need your help with."
  Say what's causing you the problem: for example, "It's difficult for me to find the right words as the subject involves your future."
- How to manage the conversation:
  Gain their **Commitment to Engage** – *Call on their strengths*, for example: "As parents who have … (express here how you've seen the good management skills they've used in the past to manage their lives, or examples from your childhood that will illustrate some of their strengths) … it's been easy for me as your son or daughter because …"
  Construct Meaning – *Be specific about the help that you need*: "I now need your help with a discussion about the future and how best to manage it."
  Start the process where you can both Converge on Agreement – *Ask for their input*: "What thoughts have you had?"

What if they object to having the conversation?

The above advice all sounds well and good, but what if they object or do not want to have the conversation?

Here you really do need to be assertive. Express your concerns assertively. For example:

> *"Mum, I'm concerned about your health; it makes me worried that I'm not seeing the care and support that's really needed. I really do need to discuss the future with you."*

Once the discussion about their future has commenced make sure that you stick to your role – help and advice only – and allow them to take responsibility for the decisions. For example if a sticking point arises, once again ask for their help:

> *"I can't make decisions about how you should run your life, nor should I. It would make me feel better though if we could go together to look at some possible assisted living facilities so that you're better informed about what choices are available. Would you be willing to humour me in that way?"*

What happens if your parents come up with a solution that you disagree with?

That's a real possibility. The question you need to answer is "Can I live with that decision?" If not, then you will have to make a very tough decision yourself – do I push my point? If so, you will need to be very assertive, for example:

> *"Dad, moving in with us is not an option. I need you to consider another alternative."*

Putting aside the consequences of this statement, notice that there is no reasoning given. If you are committed to your decision then you'll recall from the Chapter on assertiveness that giving reasons will start a totally new conversation – is this where you want to go?

CHAPTER THIRTEEN | **CONVERSATION WITH AN AGEING PARENT**

Words and phrases to avoid

You'll have noticed throughout this book that I've tried to use positive examples of what to do and say and occasionally words to avoid. However, in this Chapter I'm going to outline quite a number of negative statements (particularly openers) to avoid as I feel they are ones that many people could inadvertently consider a good way of easing into the conversation. They are not. (If you are to have a family conversation involving your siblings, this would be an excellent list to go through and discuss with them as there are some real 'howlers' here to avoid.)

What NOT to say:	Why these won't work (by now you will probably have a good idea and can reword them yourself)
• *How's the house? It must be hard to keep this place in good shape.* • *How's your health? What's the doctor saying these days?* • *How's the car? Still driving to the shops every weekend?*	These were mentioned previously. They are not really questions, rather a lead-in to the point the person wants to make. Parents will see right through them for what they are – your opinions!
• *I see the steps are a problem for you and you almost fell this morning. Is that happening a lot?*	As above – this also points out the obvious which makes no real headway in the conversation. In fact this comment may be seen as criticism. Remember, one of the needs for elderly people is independence. Note: 'You' is being used inappropriately in the past tense here and in many of the other inappropriate statements.

PART THREE | DIFFICULT CONVERSATIONS AND HOW TO MANAGE THESE

What NOT to say:	Why these won't work (by now you will probably have a good idea and can reword them yourself)
• It looks like you're "having trouble getting off the couch" or "You seem a little lonely and mixed up when you're tired". You know they say that people do a lot better where there's a lot of activity going on and things to enjoy.	Once again the speaker is expressing an opinion, not asking an open question of the parent.
• Mum said you got another speeding ticket and I noticed the rear of the car has another dent. What do you think is going on?	This will probably result in the parent speaking about the "revenue raising methods of the police" and "other fools who cannot park their cars properly". It may also lead to a nasty discussion between both parents when you have left – "Why did you dob me in, Dear?"
• I read about this man in the paper who lost control of his car and killed some kids. He was about your age. It made me think we should consider what's in your best interests with the car now.	This really does put the parent down. How would you feel if someone said this to you? (I know I'd be quite insulted.)
• Mary's parents just sold their house on Circuit Drive and moved to a retirement village – you should have heard her dad rave about not having to do any more hard work in the garden.	A third-party testimonial is not going to be heard right now no matter how well thought of Mary might be. In fact gardening could be one of their joys and something they do not want to give up.
• Remember Frank, my friend who became a doctor? He told me that his whole family has written their wills and I'm thinking we should all do that, too.	I can almost hear the parents saying (or thinking) "Huh! Is he/she/they after our money?"

CHAPTER THIRTEEN | **CONVERSATION WITH AN AGEING PARENT**

Final comment:

Remember the ultimate aim is to talk with your parents to problem-solve together, not to dictate the solution or to convince them through argument. And it's also likely that your parents will need time to come to a decision about their future – give it to them, after all they've probably given you a lot in the past.

CHAPTER 14

Giving ~~critical~~ *favourable* feedback to a friend

How can you give someone news they may not like and still remain friends?

We see something that a friend is doing or perhaps we hear about something they are going to do and we think "Oh, oh. That's probably not right", or "That doesn't sound like a good idea", or "That's going to cause (or has caused) a bit of a problem". Why do we so often avoid saying something to help them out – are we seeing something they can't? Then why not tell them?

Often we're worried about the other person's reaction: What if she gets angry? What if he cries? What if she tells me I'm an idiot? What if he gets defensive and starts blaming *me*? What if he's actually right and I make a fool of myself? And another thing that makes it hard is not knowing what to say. "How can I tell him that most other people see it differently to him?", "What words can I use that will not cause offence?", "How can I tell her such bad news and still expect her to like me?" These are hard questions to deal with – in fact it's estimated that 53 per cent of us dodge such difficult conversations.

And according to a survey by UK mediation firm Globis, 97 per cent of respondents were anxious about stress levels, 94 per cent were

CHAPTER FOURTEEN | GIVING ~~CRITICAL~~ *FAVOURABLE* FEEDBACK TO A FRIEND

worried about damaging self-esteem and 80 per cent of people were afraid of an angry response when asked about giving feedback to a friend. So it's no wonder we are somewhat reluctant when it comes to speaking with a friend about a difficult topic that may affect them and perhaps our relationship.

We may of course also subconsciously be thinking or remembering when we received some critical comments and how these affected us. Think for a moment about the last time you received some critical feedback from a friend. How did you feel? I'll bet that it wasn't an 'over the moon' feeling. No matter how right or well-intended the criticism may be we do not like to hear about our flaws, shortcomings or wrongdoings.

Here's an example of what happened when Bud Hennekes, blog owner of "A Boundless World" http://www.aboundlessworld.com/about/ received some feedback from a friend:

> *"The other day I was toying with the idea of starting a flower business by creating a website where you could buy flowers for a random person in need.*
>
> *I'd work with the flower companies to make it affordable. People could buy flowers for individuals in need of love. And I'd be helping bring smiles to hundreds of individuals. Greatest idea ever.*
>
> *While doing my research I sent an email over to my boy Sean Platt who worked in the flower industry for many years. I just knew he would love my idea and all would be merry. Eh.. not so fast.*
>
> *Long story short, Sean gave me some honest feedback.*
>
> *The jury had decided: My idea sucked.*
>
> *Whether or not I could have made the business model work is beside the point. What struck me was at how honest Sean was. Instead of lying to me and saying that it would all work out, he was frank and up front.*

> His reaction to my idea most certainly bruised my ego, but in the end he saved me hundreds of hours of hard work. [For the record I love Sean, and he wasn't overly harsh.]
>
> In today's society honest feedback is frowned upon. Criticism is almost always countered with the 'haters gonna hate' mantra. And while I too admit there are plenty of negative Nancy's of the world, I sincerely believe criticism has its place.
>
> Criticism helps us grow. Coddling does not."
>
> Bud

You can see two things from Bud's response:

- His ego was bruised
- He appreciated the honest feedback

Let's start with ego – everyone has one – and it's a very important part of our makeup. Unfortunately the word that's often associated with ego is 'big' as in "He's got a big ego". However, ego or as it's sometimes referred to, 'ego-drive', is a personal need for achievement in every endeavour: sports, education, career, life. People with a strong ego-drive are always trying to better themselves. They are motivated by challenges, opportunities and the high standards they create, so it's no wonder that when something they do or say gets a knock-back or criticism from a friend or colleague, their ego becomes dented.

As someone who is reading this book, my intuition (or 'third-ear') tells me that you have a very healthy and strong ego. Do you feel like Bud when your ego is knocked or dented? When was the last time you received some critical feedback from a friend? How did you feel? Keep this feeling in mind as we progress through the remainder of this Chapter as one of the keys to giving constructive feedback is to minimise the damage done to the other person's ego.

CHAPTER FOURTEEN | GIVING ~~CRITICAL~~ *FAVOURABLE* FEEDBACK TO A FRIEND

We're not privy to the words Bud's friend used. However, my best guess is that they were supportive, critical and honest. Let's see how that might work and why Bud appreciated his friend's honesty.

However, before we look at some words to use when giving your friend a message, let me explain that ~~critical~~ word in the heading to this Chapter. Unfortunately the words feedback, critical and bad news seem now to be synonymous. So when we hear someone say "Let me give you some feedback" or "I have some feedback for you" we know that it's most likely going to be critical, not favourable and our brain automatically goes into fight or flight mode. Therefore, I'm reframing the word 'critical' to 'favourable'. I'll go one step further: I suggest dropping the word 'feedback' altogether and depending on the situation replace it with 'advice', 'pointers', 'counsel' or 'guidance'. This is another example of reframing and while this may seem like a play-on-words or a little bit of a stretch, I have some very good reasons for suggesting we reframe feedback and use a positive, future oriented word instead:

- Feedback, although starting out as neutral (it was originally an engineering term – 'the conveyance of information fed back from an output, or measurement to an input, or effector, that affects the system') in personal communication, has now become synonymous with bad-news.
- Feedback tends to focus on the past and what has happened whereas words such as advice, pointers, guidance and so on, all refer to future actions.
- Future oriented words force us to talk about 'what might be' rather than 'what is' or 'what has been'.
- Future oriented words lead to statements that we own such as "I'd suggest that it be handled this way" rather than inferring

PART THREE | DIFFICULT CONVERSATIONS AND HOW TO MANAGE THESE

criticism such as "I think you should have …" or "Why don't you do it this way …?" or "Why did you do that?"

Along with reframing, tone of voice is particularly important when giving advice to a friend. Because they're your friend, they'll pick up very quickly on the nuances you are subconsciously communicating. So try to show concern in your tone, rather than anger (e.g. if they've done something to upset you) or frustration (e.g. if they keep doing something that annoys you) or perhaps disappointment (e.g. if you feel they have let you down). 'Concern' is a feeling that is readily communicated and understood between friends – it quickly leads to a mutual exchange of feelings.

Some guidelines for giving advice to a friend …

1. **Ask if it's OK to provide some advice**: For example,
   "Julie, I was a little concerned about our conversation yesterday with John. I'm no expert on the subject, but I do have some personal experiences to draw from. Is it OK if I offer some advice?"

   Note: This example with Julie will be built on as we progress through these guidelines. In the example, imagine that the speaker is you or I. We listened in on a conversation yesterday between Julie and John. Julie is a friend of ours and for some time we've been concerned about the words she uses when offering advice to other friends and colleagues – she uses lots of 'you' words and whilst very well intentioned, Julie's use of words often puts the other person off. So we're setting out to see if we can get the message across that Julie may have better relationships if she changes the words she uses. Follow the example and see how we go.

2. **Give advice irregularly:** If you are continually giving advice to a friend they will start to ignore what you are saying (but because

CHAPTER FOURTEEN | GIVING ~~CRITICAL~~ *FAVOURABLE* FEEDBACK TO A FRIEND

they're a friend, they will continue to listen). Pick the important things that can make a real change for your friend, rather than nit-picking. With Julie, the really important thing is to get her to change some of the words she uses as it can sometimes come across as demeaning.

3. **Act as a sounding board:** Once you've gained your friends approval to discuss the topic, ask how they see the situation. Get them to check their assumptions and why they see the situation the way they do. For example;

    "To me, John seemed to get quite upset. And I think he re-acted not only to what was said, but also to how it was said. He obviously disagreed to the opinion being given and I think there was more to it than that. What are your thoughts?"

4. **Test some tentative assumptions your friend may have:** We all make assumptions and we arrive at the best decisions when these are tested and found appropriate or found wanting and we go down another path. For example;

    "Although the suggestions sounded OK and logical to me, John didn't seem to hear them – he reacted quite strangely. Could there be another reason?" (Pause and listen: Here Julie is most likely to discuss other possible things happening in John's life – we need to shift the conversation back to the words she used, i.e. the process not the content). *What if the suggestions were put to John in a different way – using different words, or perhaps even through asking questions? How might that work? What questions would work?"*

5. **Expand their frame of reference:** One way of doing this is to ask more questions such as "What else?" or "Tell me more" or "For example?" A further useful technique is to provide some of your own experiences that may demonstrate another way, for example,

    "I think explaining it to John in another way, perhaps one that is less intimidating such as asking questions could work. I also remember going

PART THREE | DIFFICULT CONVERSATIONS AND HOW TO MANAGE THESE

to a training course where they suggested dropping the word 'you' when giving someone else some advice. Shortly afterwards, I had to give my partner Mike some really tough news – and guess what, it worked! How could the advice to John be rephrased by eliminating 'you'?"

6. **Provide process advice:** I'm sure you will now be aware that in the 'Julie' example so far, we've actually been managing the conversation process – whenever Julie started to discuss content we listened, then through questioning brought her back to the process. We now have to help Julie understand the importance of managing the process in her own conversations. For example: *"Sounds to me that you like the idea of eliminating 'you' but are a little sceptical about how it might work. Would you like to try it out on me? I'll be John and you can give me the advice without using the word 'you'. Let's see how that might work."*

7. **Brainstorm solutions:** Once you have your friend engaged in the conversation there may be an opportunity to brainstorm some other ideas that could help. Remember your opinion is not the only one and can always be improved through sharing with others.

How does that advice for Julie differ from the advice you recently received from a friend? If you now had to give similar advice to someone else, how would you give it? What words would you use?

Words to avoid

It's also worth repeating here some of the words to avoid that you're now familiar with as it's particularly tempting to drop back into old habits when giving advice to a friend:

- Avoid 'but', 'yes, but' and their first-cousins 'however' and 'although' – we've discussed these in detail in Part Two. With friends, use the 'yes, and …' alternative which is particularly relevant.

CHAPTER FOURTEEN | **GIVING** ~~CRITICAL~~ *FAVOURABLE* **FEEDBACK TO A FRIEND**

- Look out for 'You need to …' (very tempting as you probably have the answer all worked out for your friend). We've discussed the problem with 'you' in Part Two. I raise it here because with a friend, we tend to feel that we really need to help and so it's tempting to jump straight in with "You need to …" or "You should …"

Techniques to avoid

Also, if you happen to work in a commercial or government organisation, you may have heard of giving criticism or advice via the 'feedback sandwich'. This does not work. The idea behind this technique is that:

1. You start off by focusing on the strengths – what you like about the person or what they've done.
2. Then you provide the criticism – things you didn't like – the things you think they should change.
3. Lastly, you round off the feedback by reiterating the positive comments you gave at the beginning and the positive results that can be expected if the criticism is acted upon.

Sounds feasible? Unfortunately it's been found that people ignore the positive strengths mentioned in Step 1. As we've shown elsewhere in this book, they know the 'but' is coming (Step 2). It's that criticism in the middle that bites (and very salty it can be too). In Step 2 the brain has gone into 'fight or flight' mode and is not prepared to listen to anything else that follows no matter how positive. And so the final positive statements (Step 3) are also soon forgotten.

My personal experience (in receiving this type of message myself) is that it seems disparaging – the sandwich is inedible.

As Andrew O'Keeffe, author of *Hardwired Humans* says:

"The problem with the feedback sandwich is that humans have an instinctive need to classify. We classify in order to make sense and our classifications are binary in nature – on a variation of 'good' or 'bad'. So at moments of receiving feedback the listener is compelled to classify; is the feedback positive or negative? The feedback sandwich becomes a mixed message because it confuses the classification instinct."

And on the other hand, how do we manage the conversation when a friend starts to give us advice?

How do we cope when a friend starts giving us some information, advice or criticism that may be hard to accept? As an example, think about what you've already read in this Chapter – there'll be some advice you keep and some that you'll throw away – this will be similar in a conversation with a friend. However, my best guess is that no matter what, while listening to your friend you'll start to recall the things you've thought about while reading this Chapter – and that in itself will be enough for you to think rationally about what your friend is saying, no matter how effective or ineffective the words he or she is using.

So when first hearing some criticism from a friend engage your rational brain and rather than responding, ask some further questions such as:

- "When I hear xyz, what does that mean?" (Notice I did not suggest "When you say xyz what does that mean?" rather "When I hear xyz …"
- "Are there some other examples I should be aware of?"

CHAPTER FOURTEEN | GIVING ~~CRITICAL~~ *FAVOURABLE* FEEDBACK TO A FRIEND

- "What else?"
- "Tell me more"

It's known that we all react to criticism (or even well intentioned advice given in a negative way) for three reasons:
1. It may seem (to us) wrong or unfair
2. We may dislike the person giving it (unlikely in a friendship)
3. It may rock our sense of identity or security

Douglas Stone, co-author of *Thanks for the Feedback* suggests (once we're away from the conversation) to write down the nitty gritty of the message:
- "What is this feedback about and …
- What is it not about?"

Answering this two-part question will enable you to reframe the message into some positive advice – which of course you can take on-board or throw away. From previous Chapters you'll also recognise the importance of writing down your answers.

Remember, all advice has some truth in it, even if only to reveal how others think. Before dismissing it, ask yourself, "What is the nugget that I can pull out of this?"

In summary, if you have to give a friend some advice the guidelines are:
1. Ask if it's OK to provide some advice
2. Give advice irregularly
3. Act as a sounding board
4. Test some tentative assumptions your friend may have
5. Expand their frame of reference
6. Provide process advice (avoid getting caught in the content)
7. Together, brainstorm solutions

And when you get hit with some advice from a friend:
1. Stay rational (bring this Chapter to mind)
2. Get more specifics by asking questions such as "When I hear ... what does that mean?", "Are there some other examples I should be aware of?", "What else?", "Tell me more"
3. Write down answers to "What is this feedback about and what is it not about?"

Finally, when either giving advice or receiving criticism from a friend, keep in mind Bud's reaction – I'm pretty certain that Bud's friend would have done much of what's being suggested here.

Before leaving this Chapter, we should also look at what might be considered 'the other side of the coin' – giving praise.

Criticism and Praise

Are they the flip sides of the same coin? It seems not. We've seen the impact that criticism can have on friends – now what about praise? Before discussing how to give praise to a friend, it's first necessary to look at the research on the impact of praise – much of this research started with children, before focusing on adults, so let's start there.

"You're a good girl", "Gee, you did that well": these are probably things all parents have said to their children at some stage. The general idiom is that praise is good for children's development while criticism is not. However, research over the last decade or so has found that praise can also be damaging, particularly for younger children.

Researchers have found that praise for young children (perhaps up to the age of 2-3 depending on their maturity) whatever way it is given, is good for their development. However as children mature, they start to distinguish praise given for their abilities such as intelligence

CHAPTER FOURTEEN | GIVING ~~CRITICAL~~ *FAVOURABLE* FEEDBACK TO A FRIEND

(which they intuitively perceive people either have or do not have and therefore cannot be changed) compared to praise given for their level of effort or the strategies they use – these they realise can be changed.

As an early writer on the subject Haim G. Ginott said in his famous 1965 book *Between Parent and Child*:

> *"Praise, like penicillin, must not be administered haphazardly. There are rules and cautions that govern the handling of potent medicines — rules about timing and dosage, cautions about possible allergic reactions. There are similar regulations about the administration of emotional medicine."*

What are these rules for giving 'emotional medicine', i.e. praise to children?

- Be sincere and specific with your praise. As children mature, they become aware of doing things well for the praise they receive – they can in fact become 'praise junkies'. The downside of this is that if praised for similar achievements too often, they may lose interest in the intrinsic motivation of the task. The more praise children receive, the more they rely on adult evaluations instead of forming their own judgments.
- Praise only for traits they have the power to change. For example praising a child because they are 'smart' (intelligence) for example "You're a good girl", "You're so good at this", or "I'm very proud of you" reduces motivation and encourages them to compare their performance with that of others.

- Use descriptive praise that conveys realistic, attainable standards. Rather than "You're so good at this" identify what they have done well in the task, for example "I really liked the way those pieces of the puzzle were sorted into colours. That really worked well".
- Be careful about praising children for achievements that come easily to them.
- Be careful about praising children for doing what they already love to do. Intrinsic motivation (the joy of doing the task) may be lessened with too much praise.
- Encourage children to focus on mastering skills – not on comparing themselves to others.
- Avoid superlatives such as 'always' or 'never' as these either set unrealistic goals or present insurmountable barriers.

And what about praising adults: is it similar to praising children?

It seems so. We all like praise. I have to admit I think I may be a 'praise junkie', so keep those flattering emails coming in! Seriously, we all do like praise, we feel good as a result, but what else does it do?

According to Clifford Nass, author of *The Man Who Lied to His Laptop*, both praise and flattery (flattery could be described as 'praise that may be given without foundation') have more impact on our liking of the giver than of the impact on our behaviour. So praise, even of a particular achievement, will be remembered for making us feel good and for who gave it rather than exactly what is was for.

CHAPTER FOURTEEN | **GIVING** ~~CRITICAL~~ *FAVOURABLE* **FEEDBACK TO A FRIEND**

However, there may be situations where you can use praise to influence the performance of others. I've already mentioned the parental role – you may also be in a teaching, supervisory, coaching or training role. If so, the following guidelines will assist your influencing ability:

1. Tell the person in specific, descriptive terms the behaviour s/he did correctly/well <u>AND</u> the impact of that behaviour.

    Example:

    "Jill, I really like the great job you did on the Project X report for our committee I asked you to complete last week. I was especially impressed with the analysis of the numbers and the explanation of the statistics in the written part of the report."

2. Tell the person how you feel about the behaviour or how the behaviour will affect others – be specific.

    Example:

    "I'm confident the Councillors will be able to make an informed decision on our community project because of the quality of the information provided."

3. Encourage more of the same behaviour.

    Example:

    "Thanks for doing such a thorough job. Keep up the good work."

Whatever your situation, giving praise makes you feel good and the person to whom you are giving it feel good, so do keep it up. It also has an important side benefit – in giving praise you have to look for the positives in others' behaviour – and that's what this book is all about.

CHAPTER 15

The conversation you're having when you're not having a conversation

How to get what you want, really get what you want

> **HEALTH WARNING**
>
> This Chapter comes with a health warning. It includes 'How to be assertive where the stakes are high and it's either win or lose'.
>
> Use the suggestions here on 'strong assertiveness' at your own risk.

What is assertiveness? We all have our own ideas and definitions. It's a word that we often use in day-to-day conversation to describe our own or another's behaviour. One dictionary definition of being assertive is to "state with assurance, confidence or force; state strongly or positively".

And in terms of the words we use when being assertive, they vary quite considerably. There are degrees of being assertive, from using mild 'I-word' statements of requests – for example, "I would like to

CHAPTER FIFTEEN | THE CONVERSATION YOU'RE HAVING WHEN YOU'RE NOT HAVING A CONVERSATION

have ..." through to much heavier personal demands such as "I need ..." or "I must have ...".

If you read again the dictionary definition you'll see that all the words are positive 'assurance', 'confidence', 'strongly', 'positively' – with the possible exception of one – 'force'. Very strong assertiveness (perhaps forceful) is sometimes confused with aggressiveness which is quite different. True assertiveness is not crossing another's boundaries. Assertiveness acknowledges and respects the boundaries of others. Aggressiveness is disrespectful of boundaries. How can you tell the difference? Here it's our old enemy the 'you' word that gives it away – "You must ...", "You will ...", "I need you to ..." – all of these statements are asking for what we want without considering the needs of others. Excessive use of "you" is a sure-fire indicator of aggressiveness.

Before we move on to looking at how to be assertive in a positive way, it's worth doing some self-reflection to identify our natural style. A quick and easy way to do this is to answer the following question (give yourself a score from 0 = Never to 10 = Always):

When I am faced with making a choice put forward by my partner and/or friends and I have a very definite idea of the answer (or I'm sure of the action that should be taken) and they have a strong and different view, how often do I:

	0 - 10
• _Give in_ and accept the others' decisions?	
• _Ask_ for what _I want_?	
• _Tell others_ what action to take?	

That short test will give you an indication of your personal degree of being assertive. For example, if you often 'give in and accept others' decisions' then you may be more passive than assertive. After doing so, do you often think "Maybe I should have put my view forward, I really don't like this result", or "I knew it wasn't going to work out – I should have been more forceful." (I used to be a bit like that too and I know how frustrating and even self-defeating it can be.)

On the other hand if you often find yourself 'telling others what to do' then it's likely that your style will come across as very strongly assertive or perhaps even aggressive (depending on the words used and the tone of voice).

Because assertiveness is perhaps perceived as a negative trait, most often we use assertiveness when describing someone else's behaviour not ours, and the results it has on their relationships, e.g. "He's so assertive and really puts people off". So we need to delve a little deeper to get a better handle on what is meant by 'assertiveness' and how it can be used positively. 'Being assertive' is such a common phrase used to describe others' behaviour that we all have an intuitive idea of what it is and what it means when it comes to building and maintaining relationships. You can test your own interpretation of how assertiveness impacts relationships by drawing a line on the following graph. Start your line in the bottom left hand corner of the graph by answering the question:

- If a person shows this degree of assertiveness – scale from 0 (no assertiveness) to 100 (full-on assertive) – what will be the result on their relationships? You'll note that the *Relationships* axis ranges from -20 to 100, so you may for instance consider that a score of 0 on *Assertiveness* (i.e. a person never displays any assertive behaviour) actually leads to a negative impact on their relationships.

CHAPTER FIFTEEN | **THE CONVERSATION YOU'RE HAVING WHEN YOU'RE NOT HAVING A CONVERSATION**

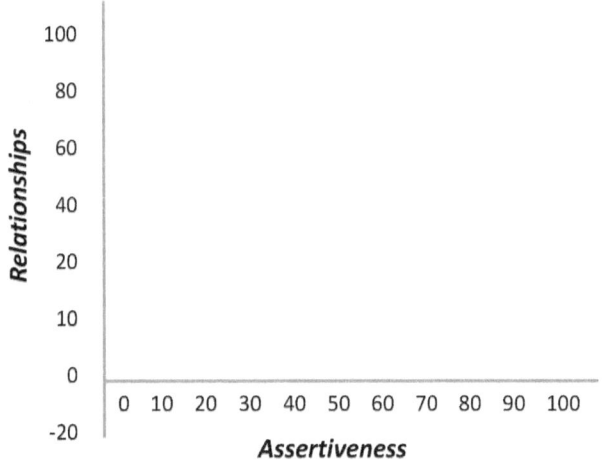

My guess (which by the way is supported by the research) is that your line will look somewhat like an inverted U. Most of us consider that displaying no or little assertiveness results in poor relationships; at the other extreme too much assertiveness badly affects our relationships, and a moderate amount of assertiveness has a positive impact on our relationships.

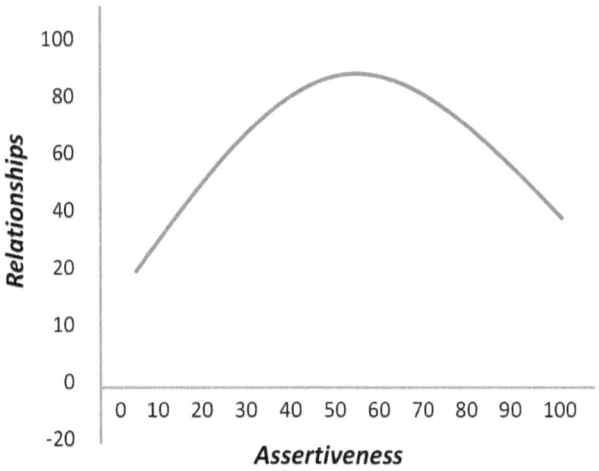

PART THREE | **DIFFICULT CONVERSATIONS AND HOW TO MANAGE THESE**

Now if I ask you to repeat the exercise with one change, i.e. to replace the *Relationships* axis with *Personal Outcomes* (i.e. the result you might get <u>other than</u> building or maintaining a relationship) you will most likely draw the line in one of two ways:

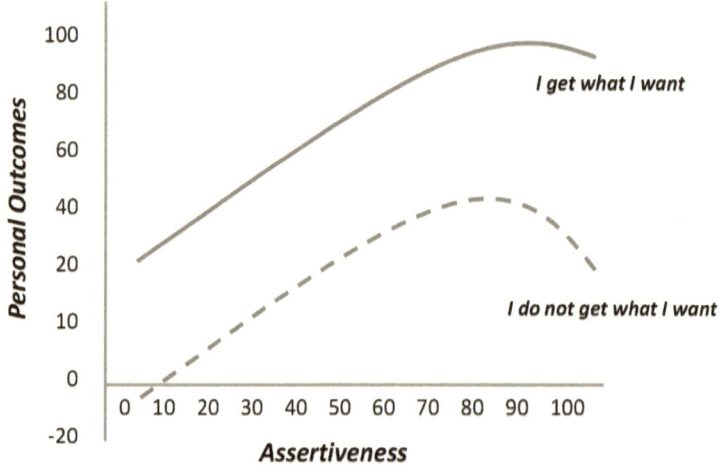

That is, when we ignore relationships and focus on our own needs, it becomes either a win/lose or a lose/lose situation.

The following is a personal example where full-on assertiveness was used to achieve a desired outcome. Some years ago my son was returning to Australia from Switzerland where he had been visiting us on a cycling holiday (at that time we were living in Switzerland). We took him to the airport in Zurich and being a Gold-Card frequent flyer, I checked him in. Everything went well – boarding pass issued, baggage checked – then we started to check-in the bike. The attendant said there would be an extra fee for the oversize bike box. That would be fine I thought: perhaps 100 francs (at time of writing 1Fr = approx. U.S.$1.05, Euro 0.95, A$1.35) would be the fee, maybe 120 francs, that would be OK. Then she said, "That will be 600 francs." You can

CHAPTER FIFTEEN | THE CONVERSATION YOU'RE HAVING WHEN YOU'RE NOT HAVING A CONVERSATION

imagine my shock (it was almost a third of his ticket cost). This is how the conversation went:

Attendant:	*"That will be 600 francs"*
Me:	*"I'm not paying it"*
Attendant:	*"I'm sorry, that's our new fee. That will be 600 francs please"*
Me:	*"I'm not paying it"*
Attendant:	*"That's in our price list, oversize bags such as bikes – 600 francs please"*
Me:	*"I'm not paying it"*
Attendant:	*"I'm sorry, that's our new fee. I must follow procedures – 600 francs please"*
Me:	*"I'm not paying it"*
Attendant:	*"I can't book the bike in without the 600 francs fee"*
Me:	*"I'm not paying it"*
Attendant:	*"I'll have to refer this to my supervisor"*
Me:	*"I'm not paying it"*
Supervisor:	*"I'm sorry Mr. Selden, but those are our new fees, the cost is 600 francs"*
Me:	*"I'm not paying it"*

Then ensued a further long series of explanations from the supervisor (including looking up their Procedures Manual), to which I only replied at every question or statement from the Supervisor:

Me:	*"I'm not paying it"*

What's happening here? You will notice:
- I only responded with my strong assertion (*"I'm not paying it"*) – this was my clearly identified need.
- At no stage did I enter into a discussion about their reason and logic. Had I done so, I had no grounds to argue – that was their fee and it was clearly outlined in their pricing schedule

Don't — *How using the right words will change your life*

and procedures. (Note: This was a new fee). My response: *"I'm not paying it"*
- I stayed entirely in 'my world' (my wants and needs) – I did not enter 'their world' (their procedures/price lists). My response: *"I'm not paying it"*

This was definitely a win/lose (personal outcome) situation and relationships did not enter into it. Who had what to gain or lose?

POTENTIAL GAINS		POTENTIAL LOSSES	
Me	The Airline	Me	The Airline
No fee	600 francs	600 francs	600 francs
My son's bike shipped	Happy Gold Card member	Bike not shipped	Unhappy Gold Card member
Happy son	Happy traveller (customer)	Very unhappy son	Lost customer (to another airline)

You could say my stance – *"I'm not paying it"* – was a gamble. And you'd be right. Because the relationship with the airline (for me) was not a big deal (I was already at their highest frequent flyer level) I was prepared to be full-on assertive and suffer the potential consequences of my son's bike not being shipped (I have to say that my son and wife who were standing with me were both really worried at this stage and later I found out, amazed at my strong assertion).

Here's the Health-Warning mentioned at the start of this Chapter: If you decide that it's a time where personal outcome is more important than the relationship, then it will always be a win/lose situation – you either get what you want or lose out, perhaps big-time depending on how you have weighed up the potential losses or gains and how much these also mean to the other party.

CHAPTER FIFTEEN | THE CONVERSATION YOU'RE HAVING WHEN YOU'RE NOT HAVING A CONVERSATION

Oh, in case you are wondering, I did not pay the 600 francs and my son's bike was shipped on the same flight as him. In this instance, my strong assertiveness worked.

If the relationship is important and you still have a strong need, want or desire to be fulfilled, then there's a softer way of being strongly assertive. For example, when my son was say six or seven and I wanted him to tidy his room, I could say:

Me:	"Chris, I need your room tidied"
Son:	"Why Dad?"
Me:	"Chris, I need your room tidied"
Son:	"Why Dad?"
Me:	"Chris, I need your room tidied"
Son:	"Why Dad?"
Me:	"Chris, I need your room tidied. I really like it when your room is tidy. Chris, I need your room tidied"

This dialogue could go on for a while yet. The key is to ensure that you stay with your needs/wants/desires. You may give your reasons (not logic – logic he can argue with, reasons he cannot) *"I really like it when your room is tidy* (my reason – 'liking'). *Chris, I need your room tidied"* but on no account get caught in either his or your logic by saying something like:

Me:	"Chris, I need your room tidied"
Son:	"Why Dad?"
Me:	"When your room is tidy, you'll be able to find things that you need very quickly" (my logic)
Son:	"But Dad, I know exactly where everything is now" (his logic)

Guess what? He's just caught me! I'm now in his world and I've got no argument – my assertion has dissipated to a very weak discussion on the benefits of having a tidy room and I'm left frustrated and with my needs unfulfilled.

There are some clear guidelines for being assertive:

1. Always state your wants, needs or desires with an 'I' statement (there's more on 'needs' in Chapter 17: When does a conversation become a negotiation?).
2. Keep your 'I' statement clean. If you want to soften the assertion, give your reasons only. Reasons are your personal opinions such as why you like or dislike something.
3. Avoid discussing logic. Logic is more scientific; it requires observable or tangible proof that something is right or wrong and can be checked by both people. You can reason with someone but you can't logic with them. Once you start discussing logic, your assertion collapses immediately.

Earlier you would have scored yourself on answering the three questions, "How often do you:

- *Give in* and accept others' decisions? – PASSIVE
- *Ask* for what *you want*? – MILD ASSERTING
- *Tell others* what action to take?" – FULL-ON ASSERTING

These describe a continuum of assertiveness and can be identified with certain words or phrases:

PASSIVE	MILD ASSERTING	FULL-ON ASSERTING
"I don't know"	"I'd like"	"I need"
"I don't care"	"I'd prefer"	"I want"
"It doesn't matter"	"I feel that"	"I must have"

Having read the discussion this far, where do you now consider yourself to be along this continuum in most day-to-day conversations?

CHAPTER FIFTEEN | THE CONVERSATION YOU'RE HAVING WHEN YOU'RE NOT HAVING A CONVERSATION

If you find that you've scored yourself more towards the passive end, then you can become more assertive:

1. Pay attention to what you think, feel, want and prefer in this conversation. Be clear on your needs.
2. Practise saying what you want particularly on things that are not that important to you or that will not damage the relationship. For example, if you see a new movie or TV show with a friend and they put forward a view (they may have really liked it), take the opposite view.
3. Remember to practise your 'I' statements – "I'd like", "I prefer" or "I feel".
4. Maintain strong and consistent eye-contact. People who assert strongly maintain eye-contact. Practise this in ordinary conversations to see how long you can maintain eye-contact before looking away – wait till the other person looks away first.
5. Remember also that your ideas and opinions are as important as anyone else's. This really helps you to be more assertive – it starts with an inner attitude that you value yourself as much as you value others.

If you find that you consider you're already reasonably assertive, but there are times when you would like to be much stronger:

1. Be very clear on what your needs are.
2. Weigh up the pluses and minuses of taking a strongly assertive stance in this situation.
3. State your needs with a strong 'I' statement.
4. Avoid being drawn into their reasoning and logic – stay with your needs.
5. If necessary, state reasons to support your needs, then return immediately to repeating your needs statement. For example,

PART THREE | DIFFICULT CONVERSATIONS AND HOW TO MANAGE THESE

"*I need your room tidied. I really like it when your room is tidy. I need your room tidied*".

6. Maintain strong eye-contact.
7. Practice these in a non-consequential situation, for example if you have to return something to a shop and the item is perfectly OK (i.e. there is no real need to return it).

If you find, or perhaps you've had some comments from others, that at times you seem to be a little overbearing or even somewhat aggressive, chances are that you're a little bit further to the right than 'Full-on Asserting' on the graph. This is most likely caused by using the 'you' word too often and too strongly when you want something from someone else – despite what others may have told you, it has nothing to do with your personality. Try these tips:

1. Be very clear on what your needs are.
2. Drop the 'you' word entirely from your statement of needs, for example avoid statements such as "You should", "You will", "I want you to", "I need you to".
3. Involve the other person in the conversation, for example, "How could this work for you?" or "What are your thoughts on the subject?"
4. Practise triangulation by using your hands, an object, paper, book etc. to direct your gaze away from the other person and encouraging them to do similarly.
5. Listen. Get into their world by working with their reason and logic. Note: Using logic here is a good strategy for someone who may be seen as overly assertive (perhaps aggressive) as it enables both of you to agree on observable or tangible proof that something is right or wrong and can be checked by both people thus providing an immediate area of agreement.

CHAPTER FIFTEEN | THE CONVERSATION YOU'RE HAVING WHEN YOU'RE NOT HAVING A CONVERSATION

Final comments:

I previously mentioned the Health-Warning in this Chapter – it can be either a win or a lose situation, particularly when it comes to relationships. In addition to the need to be mindful of the importance of relationships when deciding to be more assertive, it does require more physical and mental energy. Those who try the strong assertiveness techniques discussed here for the first time, find that it takes a lot of energy to push out their wants/needs and refrain from discussing reason and logic (which is so much easier). In fact this degree of energy is described as 'push' energy – you are pushing out (from within yourself) and quite often pushing against a contrary argument or contradictory opinion held by the other person. Be aware of this and stick with it – it will take time and practice.

CHAPTER 16

Creating an image – can a speech do it?

How to build word pictures that resonate with your audience

Although not strictly a difficult conversation, I've included this Chapter on presentations because:

a. They are often seen as difficult
b. They should make a connection (almost as if in a discussion) with your audience through the use of such techniques as rhetorical questions and metaphors
c. Everyone at some stage will have to give a presentation – even if it's a very short one at a birthday or wedding celebration – and to many people presentations are seen as challenging or difficult

Through social science research we've known for some time that the use of rhetoric, imagery and metaphor can positively impact how the audience perceives and acts on the message. However, a recent study has now taken this one step further. The results of the research by James J. Naidoo and Robert G. Lord, suggest that not only does the use of such tactics impact audience behaviour, used well they also have a positive effect on how we perceive the charisma of the speaker.

CHAPTER SIXTEEN | CREATING AN IMAGE – CAN A SPEECH DO IT?

Listen to some of the rhetoric, imagery and metaphors candidate Barack Obama used in his now (almost) famous electoral race speech in March 2008 …

> "I am the son of a black man from Kenya and a white woman from Kansas. I was raised with the help of a white grandfather who survived a Depression to serve in Patton's Army during World War II and a white grandmother who worked on a bomber assembly line at Fort Leavenworth while he was overseas.
>
> I've gone to some of the best schools in America and lived in one of the world's poorest nations. I am married to a black American who carries within her the blood of slaves and slave owners – an inheritance we pass on to our two precious daughters."

In a poll taken shortly after this speech, Obama was shown to be leading Hillary Clinton in the Democratic nomination race by 53 to 41 per cent. The behavioural impact stats are there, but did the speech impact our perception of Obama's charisma?

After winning the Democrat nomination, press reports concerning the advice being given to Obama at the time included; "Get specific – lay out concrete plans", "Describe your experience in government – make Americans comfortable with you as their CEO", "Hammer your opponent above and below the belt". None of this advice has anything to do with charisma – it is all about facts, logic and detail.

The other Presidential candidate Republican John McCain, used very little rhetoric, imagery and metaphor, but a lot of reason and logic in his speeches. For example in his address to the Los Angeles World Affairs Council in March 2008 only his opening paragraph gives any imagery or metaphor concerning McCain as a person; " … we should still shed a tear when all that is lost, when war claims its wages from us."

PART THREE | **DIFFICULT CONVERSATIONS AND HOW TO MANAGE THESE**

The remaining 34 paragraphs all talk about reason and logic, saying nothing about the character of the man. As one press report concluded; "McCain appears dependent on a teleprompter, delivering even the most personal passages with an odd detachment. In his telling, his difficult five-and-a-half years as Vietnam prisoner of war might have happened to someone else." However, McCain does do well in less formal settings such as town hall meetings and one-on-one conversations. But his discomfort behind the podium is a distinct disadvantage as he struggled for national media attention.

Initially the race between the two presidential candidates was well and truly led by Obama. Audiences loved his charisma. However, as the election race went on, the gap between the two narrowed. Audiences were now listening for what was behind the message in terms of the reason and logic that would affect their day to day lives.

The research by Naidoo and Lord supports those poll results. They say that "high speech imagery will result in higher state positive affect in followers, compared to low speech imagery". So it appears as if Obama's advisors, once the initial speech was given, were now on the right track – he'd developed an appropriate charisma in the eyes of the voting public, now it's time for reality – give them the reason and logic.

Whilst Obama's followers were encouraging him to get specific – give them the detail – look again at some of the words they themselves used to get their message across to Obama; "lay out <u>concrete plans</u>", "make Americans <u>comfortable with you</u> as their <u>CEO</u>", "<u>hammer</u> your opponent <u>above and below the belt</u>". Yes, in advising Obama to "get more specific – give them the details" – the advisors themselves were using numerous and powerful metaphors to get their message of "give them the details" across. Fascinating!

What are the messages in Naidoo and Lord's research?

192   **Don't** — *How using the right words will change your life*

CHAPTER SIXTEEN | **CREATING AN IMAGE – CAN A SPEECH DO IT?**

There are three …
1. Firstly, when speaking publicly, use *personal imagery* and *metaphors* so that the audience can see and feel your character.
2. Secondly, whilst such imagery always works well, it is most powerful when the *situation is critical* or the audience perceives they are in a crisis. People want the big picture and, in particular, to hear and feel how the speaker has lived through similar times him or herself.
3. Finally, the detail – the reason and logic – is best handled *one-on-one* and in *small group settings*. However, if you have a clear message to give in your presentation (which involves reason and logic), this will mean taking a very structured process of explicit communication as to how the big picture will translate locally or to each person in the audience.

If you have to give presentations, that's the big picture. Now what about the detail?

As this book is all about words, I'll start with some suggestions of which to use and which to avoid and conclude with a suggested format that includes metaphors, phrases and words that could be useful for your next presentation.

Of course key amongst those words to avoid is 'don't'. What other commonly used words turn people off during a presentation?

Tread carefully in your search for words. For every list of 'magic words' and 'power phrases' you might discover, you're apt to find an equally long list of overused terms to be avoided. Words like 'guaranteed' or 'unique' or 'quality' are so pervasive that your audience will tune them out altogether. Clichéd buzzwords like 'cutting edge' and 'industry-leading' or grand superlatives like 'world class' and 'once-in-a-lifetime' are better left unsaid.

PART THREE | DIFFICULT CONVERSATIONS AND HOW TO MANAGE THESE

Here are some examples of commonly used words and phrases that have lost their original meaning or impact. As you read through these see if you can replace them with a more impactful word, phrase, or better still an eye-catching metaphor. I've given some suggestions for the first three – can you provide others?

Words or phrases that have lost their impact include:	Could be replaced with …	Or a metaphor that may have a better impact …
Excellent (or excellence)	Outstanding	• This is first-rate • First class • Top notch • Blue ribbon • Five star (although this may be starting to lose some of its impact)
Awesome	Astounding	• Breath taking • Mind blowing • Hair raising • Heart stopping
Unique	Exclusive, special, unrepeatable	• One off • One of a kind • They broke the mould when they made her
Free (as in no price)		
Going/moving forward		
Like (used as a filler, particularly by teenagers)	Remove entirely. Use silence as a short spacer between sentences.	
"You know" (also often used at the end of a sentence)		

CHAPTER SIXTEEN | CREATING AN IMAGE – CAN A SPEECH DO IT?

Words or phrases that have lost their impact include:	Could be replaced with …	Or a metaphor that may have a better impact …
Basically		
Filler words such as "um", "right", "OK", or "So…".	Remove entirely. Use silence as a short spacer between sentences.	
Obviously		
No problem		
To be honest		
Stuff		
You guys		
Bucks		
Second to none		
At the end of the day		
Truth be told		
Let me share with you		
Think outside the box		
Guaranteed		
Moving forward		
Quality*		

*Quality has been included in this list to demonstrate the degree of difference of meaning the same word may have across different cultures. So for example 'quality' could mean in:

Country	Possible meaning
USA	It works
Japan	Perfection
Germany	Fit for purpose
France	Style
Australia	Service relationship

Be careful to avoid such cultural potholes – for instance with 'quality' we have a commonly used word that has different interpretations between cultures. With words such as these it would be useful to explain your interpretation of what you mean when you use such words to ensure everyone is going in the same direction.

And here are some words that are possibly on the cusp of losing their impact (!!) – What do you think?

- Impact
- Innovative
- Sustainability
- Empower
- Amazing

I'm sure you can think of some others.

Probably the best way to look at some positive words to build into your presentations is to use an example of what you mean then build in some metaphors as you construct the presentation. Please think now about the topic of your next presentation (or the last one you've

CHAPTER SIXTEEN | CREATING AN IMAGE – CAN A SPEECH DO IT?

made). As you think about your topic, use the following suggestions to develop some of the better words or metaphors to use.

For inspiration before you start, have a look at some of the metaphors and imagery that Martin Luther King Jr. used in his famous "I have a dream" speech:

- *"A lonely island of poverty in the midst of a vast ocean of material prosperity."*
- *"But we refuse to believe that the bank of justice is bankrupt."*
- *"... the quicksands of racial injustice to the solid rock of brotherhood."*
- *"... storms of persecutions and staggered by the winds of police brutality."*
- *"... a beautiful symphony of brotherhood."*

One of the reasons that Martin Luther King Jr.'s "I Have a Dream" speech is considered one of the most powerful speeches in US history is King's masterful use of the metaphor as a rhetorical device.

Take a moment to review these brilliant metaphors (I've listed them again below with space to make your comment). Even though you may not have heard or read his speech in its entirety, it's possible to glean the intent and impact of King's words.

King's metaphor:	What is he describing? What's his intent?
- "A lonely **island of poverty** in the midst of a **vast ocean** of material prosperity."	
- "But we refuse to believe that the **bank of justice** is **bankrupt**."	

PART THREE | DIFFICULT CONVERSATIONS AND HOW TO MANAGE THESE

King's metaphor:	What is he describing? What's his intent?
– "... the **quicksands** of racial injustice to the **solid rock** of brotherhood."	
– "... **storms** of persecutions and staggered by the **winds of police brutality**."	
– "... a beautiful **symphony** of **brotherhood**."	

You may have noticed in the above excerpts from his speech that King has used a pair of related metaphors to brilliantly depict cause and effect. For example in another part of his speech he compared the Emancipation Proclamation to "a great beacon of hope" and "a joyous daybreak". He was making the point that just as a beacon or daybreak can bring light and hope, the Emancipation Proclamation brought enlightenment and optimism to millions of slaves.

Below I've explored the two related metaphors with my interpretation of the point King was emphasising:

A metaphor to describe the things that are happening/not happening ...	A linking metaphor to show or describe the situation as it is now ...	The point being made ...
island of poverty	(island) *vast ocean*	The injustice of inequality between black and white Americans.
bank of justice	(bank) *bankrupt*	There is hope. This is a just society.
quicksands	(quicksand) *solid rock*	People of race will stick together to overcome all obstacles.

CHAPTER SIXTEEN | CREATING AN IMAGE – CAN A SPEECH DO IT?

A metaphor to describe the things that are happening/ not happening ...	A linking metaphor to show or describe the situation as it is now ...	The point being made ...
storms	(storm) *winds of police brutality*	The inequitable treatment of Afro-American citizens.
symphony	(singing or playing group – symphony) *brotherhood*	People of similar background will work together to overcome.

I trust some of King's imagery has given you inspiration. I'm not suggesting at this stage that you use the sophisticated 'two part' metaphor that King used in your next presentation – that's probably a little challenging. Merely begin with an easy metaphor to describe your intent – who knows, you may find that this first metaphor leads to a second, related one.

The Next Steps to delivering that fantastic speech ...

Author Cam Barber in "A short speech – create a 3 minute speech that rocks", like many presenters, uses the metaphor of a road journey. When you drive on the roads, you know where you are on those roads. Each road has a name and/or number. Each town has a name. Each house has a number. If you are at house No.100, you can go back to No.50 or forward to No.150. You can look at the signposts for directions. You can also look at your GPS for the structure of the roads in detail. In other words it's easy to navigate the roads. You cannot get lost. But when you give a presentation how can your audience know where they are? How can they know the structure of your presentation? How can they know what is coming next? They'll know because you put up signposts for them at the beginning and all along the route, so they're sure to make the final destination with you without getting side-tracked or lost.

Now let's start on that next presentation of yours (or if you've not got one coming up, review the last one you did – that will be good practice) …

1. Take your topic. As you think about your topic use the suggestions in the following table to consider the descriptive words or metaphors for inspiration (this is obviously a business presentation and the same process can also apply to your next short wedding or birthday speech).
2. The table has two columns – the first: 'Presentation phase' is a logical way of structuring the presentation to build to a strong conclusion. The second is 'Signpost language'. Think of these signs as directional aids to keep you and your audience on track so that you both arrive at your destination at the same time and with the shared knowledge and experience of the journey.
3. In the following example I've used one theme – 'marriage relationships' – for my metaphors throughout the presentation. Using a theme is not essential although it can be very effective so long as it *resonates with the audience.*

CHAPTER SIXTEEN | CREATING AN IMAGE – CAN A SPEECH DO IT?

Presentation phase:	Signpost language: Potential words, phrases or metaphors.
Write your topic here:	
1. Introduction	Here's an example of how one speaker used a metaphor in his opening remarks to deal painlessly with a very painful topic for his audience.
	After he acknowledged the group, he began: "Flying in for this meeting, I sat next to a woman with a very unusual ring on the middle finger of her left hand. When I commented on it, she said it was her wedding ring. I asked, 'Why do you have it on the wrong finger?' Replied the woman, 'I married the wrong man.'"
	After the laughter died down, the speaker then metaphorically linked the story to his point. "Given the disappointing results we have all been experiencing in the market lately, it is fair to ask, 'Are we married to the wrong man – the wrong strategy?' I believe so."
	Having eased his group into his topic and totally captured them with his off-beat opening, he then went on to present his arguments and alternative marketing strategy ideas.
What metaphor or metaphors could you use in your opening? Can you keep this as a theme throughout?	
2. Overview of the presentation	"This afternoon I'm going to explore the relationship between our product mix and our marketing strategy to see how we might save this marriage after all, they've been together a long time and I'd like to see them succeed, wouldn't you?"

Don't — *How using the right words will change your life*

PART THREE | DIFFICULT CONVERSATIONS AND HOW TO MANAGE THESE

Presentation phase:	Signpost language: Potential words, phrases or metaphors.
What metaphors could you use in your overview?	
3. Finishing a section	"It's probably fair to assume that some of you have been in relationships that didn't work out as well as expected – I know I have. The points I've raised here … are clear indicators of why our marketing strategy needs some counselling if this relationship is to flourish as it once did."
What metaphors could you use to finish a section before moving on?	
4. Starting a new section	"Now that we've seen what's causing this potential break-up in the product mix/ marketing strategy relationship, let's look at some ways we can get them back together again and engender once again the excitement we experienced when they first came together."
How could you relate the new section to the one you've just finished?	
5. Analysing a point	• "Where does that lead us and how should we foster the relationship?" • "Let's consider this in more detail and see how the marriage might work … " • "What does this mean for them, for us?"

CHAPTER SIXTEEN | CREATING AN IMAGE – CAN A SPEECH DO IT?

Presentation phase:	Signpost language: Potential words, phrases or metaphors.
What are the key points you want your audience to remember? How could you use a metaphor (or your theme) to reinforce these points?	
6. Paraphrasing, clarifying and giving examples	• "A good example of how our marketing strategy and product mix can really hit it off is … " • "As an illustration, when they are really working in harmony, sharing the load and working towards the same outcomes … " • "To show how this new relationship could really gel … "
What are the examples that will resonate with your audience?	
7. Summarising and concluding	"In conclusion, if we were to listen in on the conversation between the marketing strategy and the product mix, what would we hear? What would they be saying to one another? Would they be describing a match made in heaven? (Pause) I'm sure we'd hear things like … Together, let's reinforce those remarks"
What do you want your audience to remember? To do? How can you link your conclusion with your opening metaphor?	

A final comment:

You'll have noticed in the example given that the speaker has used 'we' in his opening remarks. Why was he justified in jumping straight to 'we' without going through the 'I' and 'you' phases first as was discussed in Chapter 7? Was there a shared understanding of the issue or problem? Look at his words once again, "Given the disappointing results we have all been experiencing in the market lately". Obviously this is common knowledge to his audience and is the reason for this meeting, hence his legitimate use of 'we' – we have a shared problem.

However, in his next statement he reverts to 'I' – "Are we married to the wrong man, the wrong strategy? *I* believe so." He's now giving his personal opinion which is yet to be tested, justified and accepted by his audience. He needs to gain the audience's acceptance so at the moment it's only his opinion as to the reasons for the poor market results.

He will then go on to lead his audience through his reasoning (with facts and logic) and engender their support with rhetorical questions and metaphors. He's thus sticking to the appropriate use of 'I', 'you' and 'we'.

Can you also see how he followed the conversation process?
1. Open a Channel – create a welcoming space
2. Commit to Engage – create value for the audience
3. Construct Meaning – find common ground
4. Converge on Agreement – search for areas of agreement
5. Evolve – what's changed – Actions? Beliefs? Ideas?
6. Act or Transact – what will happen next?

CHAPTER SIXTEEN | CREATING AN IMAGE – CAN A SPEECH DO IT?

Consider how you can use metaphors to guide your audience through your next presentation – whether it be a wedding speech, birthday celebration, committee address or board presentation – with a clear and visual road map and signposting so that everyone arrives home 'tired but happy'.

CHAPTER 17

When does a conversation become a negotiation?

Tips to improve success in all negotiations

When you left home for work this morning or you got up to take the kids to school or you took yourself off for that cappuccino with friends, did you feel ready to face the day knowing that you were going to have a number of successful negotiations? Chances are the word "negotiation" never entered your head. Perhaps it should have!

We often think of negotiation as a formal process conducted behind closed doors by high powered executives, politicians or world leaders. Yet every day all of us negotiate. You may have to agree with colleagues on the content of a report or presentation; with a customer over a disputed invoice; with a plumber or electrician on the terms for services; with a neighbour over the state of a fence; or with your partner on what to have for dinner tonight or perhaps where to go on the weekend. All of these conversations are negotiations – where the two (or more) of you, your partner, your friends, your colleagues – have to agree on a decision to take action.

CHAPTER SEVENTEEN | WHEN DOES A CONVERSATION BECOME A NEGOTIATION?

Unfortunately we don't recognise these situations as negotiations nor ourselves as negotiators. As a result we often enter these discussions less prepared than we could be. The result? Sometimes a less-than-successful outcome.

To help make all your daily negotiations more successful (for both you and the other person) you need to use the right words, follow a good negotiating process and take on the attitude that "I am a negotiator".

In terms of the right words — we've covered these earlier in the book — it's merely a matter of using them appropriately and following a sound negotiating process — the key is to be prepared to negotiate. To do so, you'll need to be clear on the following:

- State your case clearly and appropriately — "What is it that I really want from this negotiation?" Try and quantify what it is you want, i.e. amount of time, money, resources, services, etc.
- Organise your facts — "How will I support my case?" — "What facts do I have that will support what and why I want what I do?"
- Control the timing and pace of your discussion.
- Properly assess both your and the other person's needs. These needs are non-negotiable, i.e. how you want to feel as a result of a successful negotiation.

How do you carry out these four points successfully? First, you need an understanding of some of the key principles of successful negotiating. Try this quiz to test your knowledge of negotiating by answering 'True' or 'False' to each of the following five questions:

PART THREE | **DIFFICULT CONVERSATIONS AND HOW TO MANAGE THESE**

	TRUE	FALSE
1. I should ask for twice the amount I need		
2. My aim is to prevent the other person from saying "No"		
3. A small concession will relieve the pressure on me		
4. A "Win/Win" result is always possible		
5. Admitting to an error or omission is a sign of weakness		

The following answers will provide some useful tips for your day-to-day negotiating situations.

1. Should I ask for twice the amount I need? *False.*

If you do, you'll undoubtedly have to back down and will lose an important opportunity to influence the other person. Research clearly indicates that negotiators who make large concessions end up worse off. The secret of successful negotiating is to first identify your needs then work out a range of options that will satisfy those needs. Start the negotiation by asking for the options that best meet your needs (the negotiation experts call these options 'wants', i.e. what we want – I'm using 'options' and 'wants' interchangeably here).

What are needs?

'Needs' are those (often) hidden things that drive us to achieve – they cannot be seen or touched, but they are always felt. They are often

CHAPTER SEVENTEEN | WHEN DOES A CONVERSATION BECOME A NEGOTIATION?

hard to describe, such as the love that comes with a good relationship or the feeling of security when one is well paid.

Needs should be clearly distinguishable from 'wants'. Wants are the physical things that we can see, touch and describe, such as the hug between two people in love or the description of a $150,000 salary package to make one feel very secure. Wants are the things that we get that satisfy our inner needs. This distinction between needs and wants is very important. To understand this clearly is to understand effective negotiating.

Needs are never negotiable – after all they are what drive us to want 'things'. Wants on the other hand are always negotiable. So for example you might like a hug (want) to gain affection (need) but you will sometimes settle for a peck on the cheek (an alternative to the original want) or holding of hands (another alternative to the original want) or even a pat on the back (another alternative want) to satisfy your need for affection.

So to summarise this example of the distinction between needs and wants:

Your original **'need'** in this example is **'affection'**.

This could be satisfied by (at least) four **'wants'**:

- a hug
- a peck on the cheek
- holding of hands
- a pat on the back

Now if you have a need for affection from your partner, what other wants (ways of displaying the need for affection) could you ask for? Try to write out three or four here:

My 'need' for affection from my partner could be satisfied by some of the following 'wants'

PART THREE | **DIFFICULT CONVERSATIONS AND HOW TO MANAGE THESE**

_____

_____

_____

_____

Important note: Your original need for affection is always non-negotiable. How you satisfy that need (through a variety of wants or options) is always negotiable.

How do you decide on what your needs are?

If your needs are not readily evident (unlike in our affection example between a couple), then the best way to be clear about your needs is to ask the question "Why?" when you think about what you want and keep answering it till you find something that you can't see or touch. For example, let's say that you decide you want a new car – ask the question:

- "Why do I want a new car?"
- *Answer: "To get to work".*
- "Why do I want a new car to get to work?"
- *Answer: "To save money. The old one's costing a lot to run"*
- "Why do I want to save money?"
- *Answer: "I need to feel secure that I have some money in the bank for unexpected expenses."*

Notice in this final answer the word "feel" appears as does "need" – "I need to feel secure". In most cases when you find an answer to "Why?" that includes the word "feel" you'll know that you've uncovered

CHAPTER SEVENTEEN | WHEN DOES A CONVERSATION BECOME A NEGOTIATION?

your need. So in this example by continually asking "Why?" you've identified your need as "to feel secure (about money)". So now you can look at a number of further options to satisfy that need for financial security such as:

- Catching public transport to work
- Getting a ride with a friend or colleague
- Getting a ride with a friend part of the way and walking the rest
- Riding a bike to work

All of these options will save the initial outlay on a car plus running expenses which will satisfy your need for financial security. Some have added benefits such as health (walking, riding sharing with a friend (companionship) and so on).

Shortly I'll describe some of the words you can use in an effective negotiation to identify a range of wants that will enable you to satisfy your needs. But first, back to that true/false quiz …

2. Is your aim to prevent the other person from saying "No"? *False.*

In fact getting a "No" from the other person can be very useful because it gives you the opportunity to ask "Can you give me your reasons?" This leads to uncovering the other person's real needs and some options that will satisfy them – options which you can probably supply.

One aim of negotiating is to create a massive list of options that will satisfy your needs and do the same for the other person. In this way both of you are likely to come up with some options that will satisfy each person. Some questions that will help you develop these options are:

- "What other options might be available?"
- "When I hear 'that can't be done' may I ask why?"
- "If there were no limitations (to what's being suggested), what would a successful solution look like to you?"
- "From what I've heard it appears that it may not be possible to ... at this time. What could make it possible?"
- "In an ideal world what options would satisfy your needs?"
- "Can you give me an indication of how that might work?"
- "How could I help to ... ?"

3. Will a small concession relieve the pressure? *False.*

If you make a small concession, chances are you are negotiating over options rather than needs. Additionally, the other person may think you are weakening and put more pressure on. Far better to state or restate your needs and then explore as many options as possible to satisfy them. As part of this negotiation you may come back to the offer that was just rejected, or you may find some even better options. Either way you have gained a lot more information and not weakened your case.

As Roger Fisher and William Ury, authors of the ultra-best-selling *Getting to Yes: Negotiating Agreement Without Giving In* point out:

> "Soft negotiators ... want to avoid personal conflict, make concessions readily and reach an amicable resolution. They are often exploited and feel bitter afterwards."

So instead of making a small concession, ignore the current option and refocus on finding options that will satisfy your needs. For example:

CHAPTER SEVENTEEN | **WHEN DOES A CONVERSATION BECOME A NEGOTIATION?**

- "I need to have (express here your inner <u>need</u>, not one of your wants). What options can you suggest that will help me in satisfying my <u>need</u>?"

Note: In this example the word 'need' has been used twice. Once you've established your need and if possible before negotiating, write out your need in a simple and clear statement. Then state and restate this as you negotiate. For example if you are negotiating with your partner about what to do on the weekend, you may find that you've had a tough week and you really need to feel 'up-beat' on the weekend, so you could state your need as,

- "What are we doing on the weekend? I've really had a tough week and I need to feel up-beat." Your partner might suggest "Let's play a round of golf", to which you could say "Golf's good for exercise and it sometimes gets me frustrated, so that's not a real option – what else could you suggest that will make me feel up-beat?"

In this example, be careful to stick with your need to feel 'up-beat' and avoid discussing the merits of golf (which is only one option). Stick with your need to feel "up-beat" and continue to search for more options. Such a discussion will most likely result in activity that both of you will enjoy and satisfy your needs to feel "up-beat".

4. **A "Win/Win" result is always possible.** *False.*

It's desirable, but not always possible. Sometimes even the best negotiators have to "agree to disagree". The way to improve your ratio of "Win/Wins" is to focus very clearly on your own real needs (not positions or wants) and the needs of the other person. Searching for many different options to satisfy both people's needs generates more "Win/Win" situations.

For example, there's a story about two sisters arguing over an orange. There's only one orange left in the fruit bowl and both sisters have determined that they want it, and cannot possibly do without it. They become so aggressive about the situation that at one stage they even come to blows. Eventually they decide that since they cannot agree over who should have the orange, they will cut it in half. Having cut the orange in half the two sisters turn away, both completely unsatisfied with the outcome. Although each got half the orange, it's a clear case of Lose/Lose.

As you've probably gathered by now this could become a Win/Win if both sisters were to focus on needs rather than options. Why did each want the orange? All it would have taken was for the sisters to take time out from screaming at each other, "I want it!", and instead asked each other one simple question, "What do you want the orange for?" This question would have uncovered that the first sister was thirsty, and needed the juice from the orange to quench her thirst. The second sister, on the other hand, wanted to bake a cake and wanted the rind and flesh of the orange for her cooking – she needed to feel the respect from her mother for baking such a great cake. As is often the case, something so simple could have saved so much agony.

Note: A more experienced negotiator instead of asking "What do you <u>want</u> the orange for?" would ask "What do you <u>need</u> the orange for?".

5. Is admitting to an error or omission a sign of weakness? *False.*

Research shows that disclosing such information demonstrates honesty. In psychological terms, it breeds what is called "reciprocity" –

CHAPTER SEVENTEEN | WHEN DOES A CONVERSATION BECOME A NEGOTIATION?

if you do something for me then I'll do something for you. People are far more likely to be honest with you when you are honest with them. Pulling the wool over someone's eyes may give you a short term result at the expense of a long term relationship.

One classic example of how powerful admitting an error or an omission can be, is the impact the word "sorry" has on the other person. 'Saying sorry' and 'admitting error' can be a breakthrough in the negotiation particularly when emotions are running high. Saying 'sorry' works because it helps soften entrenched positions where those powerful, unstated personal needs are blocking willingness to move forward.

There was a report in the press some time back about a British couple who hold the record for the world's longest marriage. They claimed their success over 80 years was based on a glass of whisky, a glass of sherry and the word 'sorry'. They said the real secret of their time together was that "you must never be afraid to say 'sorry'."

Finally, four tips to help you negotiate successfully:

- *If you want a better deal, ask for one.* You'll never know unless you ask! Remember, make sure it will satisfy your needs – avoid getting locked into bargaining over positions.
- *Argue to learn, not to win.* To meet your own needs you need to learn as much as possible about the other person and their needs. The more you learn the better chance you have of getting a good deal (for both people).
- *Make proposals regularly during the negotiation.* Proposals move the negotiation forward. Use proposals such as "If you will

provide … then I might consider … ." The other person's response to these proposals will give you a lot of information to work with.
- *Ask for, and give, as much information as possible.* For example questions such as "Can you explain your reasons for … . ?', "What are your priorities?" and "What else is there that you think I should know?" are excellent ways of gathering the information you need.

Successful negotiating!

CHAPTER 18

Conversation titbits

How to overcome conversation stoppers and improve conversation deepeners

1. How to counter someone who talks over the top of you

During a discussion on diversity in technology at the South by Southwest Music, Film and Interactive Conference (Austin, Texas 2015), Google executives Eric Schmidt and Walter Isaacson were criticised for talking over US Chief Technology Officer Megan Smith.

An audience member asked: "Given that unconscious bias research tells us that women are interrupted a lot more than men, I'm wondering if you are aware that you have interrupted Megan many more times?" Ironically the asker was head of Google's Unconscious Bias Team, Judith Williams.

According to a study by Adrienne Hancock and Benjamin Rubin at the George Washington University, women do get interrupted more than men and surprisingly when the speaker is a man or a woman in equal numbers. Whilst women will readily relate to this phenomenon of being interrupted I'm sure there will be many men reading this who also find being 'talked-over' frustrating.

There are at least two strategies you could take in such instances:
- Be assertive

  OR
- Go with their story and steer them towards yours

If you decide to **take the assertive approach**, remember from Chapter 15 on assertiveness there are three clear guidelines:
1. Always state your wants, needs or desires with an 'I' statement (and of course avoid 'you')
2. Keep your 'I' statement clean –
   "Can I please have a moment to finish what I'm saying?"
3. Avoid discussing logic – restate your reasoning –
   "I've clearly heard that point, now here's what I think"

And should you decide to go the assertive route be mindful that it may affect the relationship to some extent. You'll recall from our discussion on assertiveness that it requires a good deal of 'push' energy and is likely to provoke a push back from the other person.

Should you decide to **work with their point** and **guide them towards yours**, psychotherapist Diane Bath who frequently deals with patients expressing their frustration at being talked-over suggests five tactics. These are summarised as:
1. First, listen. Make sure you know what the person is talking about and their key point or message. If they are an incessant interrupter, then just interrupting them back will only exacerbate the level of emotion in the conversation. Both voices will rise in volume and stances will become more erect – you have now entered the 'stand up and fight' mode.
2. After listening for a short time and working out what they are trying to communicate, ask them for permission to interrupt …

CHAPTER EIGHTEEN | CONVERSATION TITBITS

- *"May I interrupt you there?"*

OR

- *"Can I please have a moment to finish what I'm saying?"*

OR

- *"Excuse me Pete, I didn't get to finish what I'm saying. I'd like to add that ..."*

Note: In these last two examples the words "what I'm saying" are used rather than "what I was saying". This ensures that the other person hears (subconsciously) that you are still speaking in the present tense and is therefore more likely to accept the interruption as a natural flow to the conversation.

3. When you interrupt be ready to say something about what you hear them saying. If it's possible, try to find something positive about what they're saying or about them. This shows that although you are trying to stop them, you have listened. For example,
   - *"Wait, I'd like to finish my thought now"* then add what you were going to say about them.

4. Add some experience of your own that will confirm that you understand what they're experiencing. For example a similar event, a similar feeling or a funny story – anything that gives you a chance to share your own experience and that you can tie to theirs. Although they are interrupting you, this tactic cultivates common ground and is more likely to encourage reciprocity.

5. Stop the conversation if it goes on too long. After all it's your time they are using. For example,
   - *"I need to move on now – can we finish this conversation tomorrow (or when you have time)?"* And at this point you may also need to revert to the assertive approach mentioned earlier.

Because interrupting happens to all of us from time to time, we've probably used one of the following inappropriate phrases, sentences or questions to overcome it. These suggestions will give you an opportunity to improve your responses:

Inappropriate response to the interrupter ...	A better way to stop the interrupter ...
"You're speaking over me. Please don't."	"May I have a turn to speak?"
"You're talking over me."	"Can I please have a moment to finish what I'm saying?"
"You always butt in."	"May I comment on what's been said so far?"
"You are always cutting me off."	"I'd like a few moments to finish what I was saying"
"You talked over me when I was trying to tell you about my sister. I feel like you haven't really heard what I've tried to say about her situation."	"I really need to explain my sister's situation. When I'm finished explaining, I'd like to hear your ideas"

You'll notice the use of 'you' that makes these statements/questions inappropriate and how using 'I' changes the tone, yet still remains assertive.

Note: 'may' and 'can' although often used interchangeably in everyday conversations, have quite different meanings. 'May' is a request to be allowed to do something, whereas 'can' refers to your ability to be able to do something. So for example "May I interrupt?" asks for permission whereas "Can I interrupt?" is asking the other person "Do I have the skill to interrupt (you)?" However, 'can' does seem stronger; for example "Can I interrupt you there?" appears almost as an assertive declaration rather than "May I interrupt you there?" which is more passive (and perhaps polite). Because of its apparent strength and although not always grammatically correct, I'd recommend using 'can' in most cases.

2. How to handle questions that aren't really questions

"Don't you think …" or "Don't you think you should …?" are typical examples. The Free Dictionary describes "Don't you think …" as "a vague statement of negation (more polite or gentle than simply saying "no")."

Although this type of statement is phrased as a question (including the upward inflection at the end), it is not. It's a directive. It's a statement of the speaker's opinion and often given as contrary to what the other person has just put forward or suggested. My experience is that these are not particularly destructive to the conversation; however, they can become annoying if heard continually. A suggested way of handling these is to:

1. Answer with a question:
   - "Am I hearing that … I should do … is that correct?"
   - "Tell me more …"
   - "Can you give me an example of what you mean?"
2. Once you've heard their point, follow with another question to direct the conversation back to you. For example:
   - "How does that relate to what I'm proposing?"
   - "How would that work with what I'm suggesting?"
   - "How would you see my idea working with what you're suggesting?"

These follow-up questions force the speaker to consider carefully your point of view and not dismiss it out of hand. They will lead to a constructive discussion between the two of you.

3. Enriching one word exclamations such as 'awesome'

Is it my imagination or are descriptions of things of beauty or terror becoming much shorter and less imaginative? For example the word 'awesome' has become an overused adjective intended to denote something as 'cool' or 'great' but instead winds up meaning 'lame'. This is often a reflection of the lameness of the person using the word and is a definite conversation stopper.

One way of enriching the subsequent conversation when hearing one-word exclamations such as 'awesome' is to ask:

- "When I hear 'awesome' I'm not sure what it actually means. Can you explain why this … is awesome?"
  OR
- "Why is this … awesome?"

4. Common stoppers that may not seem like stoppers at the time

- "That sounds great. I'll let you know"
- "No, it's fine (or OK, good, right etc.)"
- "I really like that, but …"

These (and others that you can probably recall) are all negations. The best way of dealing with these is to retort in the positive, such as when you hear:

CHAPTER EIGHTEEN | CONVERSATION TITBITS

- "That sounds great. I'll let you know" → *"What part of it sounds great to you?"*
- "No, it's fine (or OK, good, right etc.)" → *"Why/how is it fine?"*
- "I really like that, but …" → *"What is it that you really like about …?"*

You'll notice in all of these the response picks up the positive part of the speaker's statement and reflects it back to them as a question. This forces them to focus on the positive aspects of the topic or subject.

5. And here are some conversation stoppers you should avoid

- *"Let me see what I can do"*
    Now there's nothing wrong with this statement apart from the fact that it tends to close off further discussion. Depending on the situation, this may be quite appropriate. So what's the downside? If you find yourself using this statement a lot, then there's a very good chance that you are taking on many problems that could or should belong to someone else to solve. If this does resonate with you then one way of overcoming this is to ask questions that will get the speaker involved in the solution such as:
    – "How do you intend to handle this?"
    – "What are the next steps you'll be taking?"
    – "Who do you intend to discuss this with?"
- *"Let me be honest"* or *"Let me be perfectly honest with you"* or *"To be honest"* or *"I'll give you my honest opinion"* or *"To be brutally honest"* or *"Let me be truthful"*

The listener will often think, "Do these mean that you haven't been honest with me in the past? Or that I should disregard everything else that you say because this is the truth?" You could be quite sarcastic and respond, "Finally, some honesty!" Not recommended.

It's been found that people turn off and stop listening; they hear these and classify the speaker as untrustworthy. So if any of these statements that use the word 'honest' or 'truth' are amongst your usual sayings, I'd suggest dropping them.

There are many of these types of phrases (such as "Don't take this the wrong way" or "To tell you the truth") that we use regularly – the experts call them 'qualifiers' or 'performatives', and they can become quite habitual. Often we do not realise we are using them. Yet when reading them in text they seem quite straightforward; for example, "as far as I know…". However, when spoken they are almost always followed by a statement that signals bad news or even dishonesty, for example, "as far as I know it's not possible to do that", and have shown to heighten a sense of uneasiness in the listener.

James W. Pennebaker, Chair of the Psychology Department of the University of Texas, was quoted in the *Wall Street Journal* recently as saying these phrases are a form of dishonesty:

> "Essentially, taken alone, they express a simple thought, such as 'I am writing to say…' At first, they seem harmless, formal, may be even polite. But coming before another statement, they often signal that bad news, or even some dishonesty on the part of the speaker, will follow."

Following is a list of these qualifiers and why they might be conversation stoppers; or why they might be merely annoying, or

perhaps why they could even be dangerous. I've grouped them into three categories – Phrases or Questions that:
1. may be harmful to the conversation or hazardous to the ongoing relationship
2. are less dangerous, but should be avoided wherever possible
3. are not harmful nor dangerous, but may be heard as ineffectual by the listener.

Conversation stopper ...	What they really mean and why they should be avoided:
1. These phrases/questions may be harmful to the conversation or hazardous to the ongoing relationship:	
"Can I be ... ('frank', 'direct', 'honest')?"	See our earlier discussion on 'honest'. Avoid.
"No offence, but" or "I hate to be the one to tell you this..." or "Don't take this the wrong way" (often followed with 'but')	Of course what follows these statements is going to be hurtful or offensive. Always own your own opinion – not others'. You could say for example "I've heard that ..." or "I've seen that ..."
"With all due respect"	Recipients often think *"You're setting me up to be disrespected"*. People see straight through this as hollow words. This is a phrase that is often used by politicians.
"Frankly"	*"So, you think I'm a dummy or less intelligent!"*
"I want you to know ..."	Often taken by the listener as overbearing.
"I hear what you're saying ..."	You'll recall this one from Chapter 7; *"I hear what you say but I disagree with it so totally that I am not even going to bother considering it. In fact I have already forgotten it. Here's what I think ..."* Drop from your conversation entirely.

PART THREE | DIFFICULT CONVERSATIONS AND HOW TO MANAGE THESE

Conversation stopper ...	What they really mean and why they should be avoided:
"I'm not trying to hurt your feelings, but ..."	The only part of this phrase the listener will hear is *"hurt your feelings"*. If it is bad news and you do need to apologise for it, you could say *"I'm sorry. This is tough news for me to give"*.
"Confidentially ..." OR "Can I tell you this in confidence?"	This is similar to 'honesty'. Be careful as this phrase puts pressure on the listener. Do you want to go to this extent?
"Actually ..."	Interrogation experts suggest when people answer a question such as *"What did you do on the weekend?"* those who prefix their answers with 'actually' are more likely to be lying about what follows. (I heard a five-minute community presentation recently where the speaker used 'actually' 23 times!)
2. The following are less dangerous, but should be avoided wherever possible:	
"I may be wrong, but" OR "If I didn't know better"	Means *"I am right"*. Try to avoid these as they sound demeaning.
"I'm just saying ..."	Generally used as a defence mechanism when you question the speaker about their opinion. Although it's an 'I' statement it will be seen as defensive. Better to use *"I believe"* or *"I suggest"*.
"I don't mean to be rude, but ..."	Once again the only word the listener will hear is 'rude' – Do you really want to be seen as 'rude'?
"Promise me you won't get mad, but ..."	What you really mean here is *"You're going to get really mad."*
"It's really none of my business, but ..."	Means *"I'm probably going to butt in to something that's none of my business"* so why not avoid it all together?
"It really doesn't matter to me, but ..."	If it doesn't matter, then why say it?
"Nothing personal!"	Of course it's personal! Why else would you say it?

CHAPTER EIGHTEEN | **CONVERSATION TITBITS**

Conversation stopper ...	What they really mean and why they should be avoided:
3. Nothing too wrong with the following, they just seem ineffectual:	
"It is what it is"	Superfluous.
"I am thinking that ..." OR "As far as I know ..."	Nothing really wrong with these, only that they are qualifiers and weaken the statement to follow. If you need to show strength, change to *"I propose"* or *"I recommend"* or one that's a little softer, *"I suggest"*.

In summary **Conversation Stoppers** can be any of the following:

- Using qualifiers or performatives which at best weaken your statement and at worst may make you seem dishonest
- Accusing the speaker of negative intent (even if they haven't finished speaking)
- Taking over the conversation
- Changing the subject (too often)
- Refusing to let someone speak (remember, most of us regularly interrupt the speaker before he or she finishes)
- Going off on tangents
- Teasing and sarcasm
- Arguing
- Lack of curiosity (disinterest can bring a quick halt to any conversation)
- Questions that make people feel judged or shamed
- Questions that aren't questions, but directives (e.g. "Don't you think you should ...")

PART THREE | **DIFFICULT CONVERSATIONS AND HOW TO MANAGE THESE**

6. Conversation deepeners – how to take your conversations to the next level

If you want some examples of how to improve a conversation, try using what have been termed **'Conversation Deepeners'**:

- Let the speaker know you're listening by nodding, making eye contact and asking questions to make sure you understand him/her.
- Draw people out by asking open-ended questions that invite expansive answers – "What else?"
- Explore the language people use and the thinking behind their statements – "Tell me more" "For example?" "For instance?"
- Ask questions that are constructive, resource-seeking and forward-moving. For example, ask about hopes and positive achievements, rather than mistakes or regrets.
- Ask someone to say more about the things he/she finds meaningful – "That seems really important to you. Tell me more."
- Ask questions that invite the speaker to go beyond 'black and white' thinking by exploring complexity – "That seems really comprehensive. What's your thinking behind that?"
- Ask 'think' questions – "What do you think about …" to delve into what the person is thinking about the topic and 'feel' questions – "How do you feel about …" to uncover how the other person is feeling about the topic.
- Use 'and …' followed by the other person's metaphor to understand how he or she is feeling.

7. How to defuse an argument

Arguments are caused when either or both people become emotional over a difference of opinion (could be fact or fiction – doesn't matter). The key to defusing an argument is to get the emotional level of both people down and have them discuss their differences rationally.

Now that you've read this far, it almost goes without saying that 'depowering' your emotions starts with using the right words and avoiding others, for example,

To avoid:
- "Don't you think …"
- "You" – never use in the past tense
- "But" and "Yes but"

To use:
- "I" statements
- Slow delivery of words, phrases and sentences
- Lower tone of voice
- Non-threatening and open questions
- Listening more than speaking
- 'and' statements, particularly picking up on any metaphors they are using

Once your emotional levels are lowered, it also has a calming effect on the other person.

Some other helpful tips include:
- Summarise the points where you already agree – finding common ground is important.
- Once you've summarised the points where you agree, do the same for the main point of the argument as well – where you

differ. Let the other person know that you really do want to understand their point.
- Use the 'Let's swap sides for a moment' tactic. Ask the other person to summarise your argument and you do the same for theirs. For example, "Let's swap sides for a moment. If you were in my shoes, what would you do/say?"
- Use the triangulation method to discuss the main point of the argument.
- Remember the power of saying 'sorry' if you've done something wrong.

8. Finally, that conversation you have with yourself

I was having coffee recently with a friend and discussing some of the topics I'm working on for this book when she said "You know, Bob, I often have a conversation with myself – will you include that?" Now I know she wasn't talking about 'talking to yourself' in a derogatory way as we sometimes do, she was talking about that 'voice in our head' that we use regularly to 'discuss' what we are doing, have just done or are going to do. We all do it, but how often do we consciously consider what we're saying to ourselves? For most of us it's merely background chatter and probably often negative such as:

- "I wish I hadn't said that"
- "I'm not sure I can do this"
- "I'm too busy to do what I'd really like to do"

When you catch yourself with that negative thought, try the following:

CHAPTER EIGHTEEN | CONVERSATION TITBITS

1. Replay the thought in the positive. If you've ever watched a top flight tennis match you'll notice that the best players always 'replay' (as an air swing) a shot they've just miss-hit in the way they should have played it, thus providing the brain with a positive image for the next time they need to play a similar shot. So for example you could 'replay' "I wish I hadn't said that" to "Next time I'm in a similar situation, I'm saying '… … …'".
2. Find a positive example of how something can be done. For example, if you're starting to question yourself about taking on a difficult task *"I'm not sure I can do this"*, try thinking back to times when you have been successful at similar tasks. Or if you've not had that positive experience, try seeking out people similar to yourself who have been successful. For instance you may be thinking about a lifestyle change – *"I'm too busy to do what I'd really like to do"* – so you could surf the net to find examples of people similar to you who have done what you'd really like to do.

The conversation you have with yourself goes on whether you are aware of it or not. You can use it to your advantage by becoming more aware of it and using this 'conversation' to program your brain with the positive thoughts, words and actions that will make you a more positive person.

I've spent a good deal of time and effort researching and writing this book on 'getting the words right when in conversation with others' only to realise that probably the most important conversations we have are with ourselves. Make yours great!

Conclusion

Don't: How Using the Right Words Will Change Your Life

Are your words holding you back or moving you forwards?

Most of what I've learned about words, language and communicating was more by accident than by intent. I was simply curious enough to go poking around trying to figure things out. In doing so, I've come across some of the key themes in this book.

I've now used all the 'rules', techniques and tips outlined in this book for many years in my role as a husband, parent, sports coach, manager and trainer – and they work! That's not to say that I get it right every time, but it does give me a flying start to having many positive conversations. I trust that this book has provided some new tips for you or at the very least confirmed some of the things you are already doing. My final thought provokers for you:

- *What are you now applying? How is it working?*
- *What words are you using more often? What words are you avoiding?*
- *And what about those difficult conversations? How are they being managed?*

CONCLUSION | **DON'T – HOW USING THE RIGHT WORDS WILL CHANGE YOUR LIFE**

Here's a summary of what's been covered:

***The "don't" rule* ... (Chapter 1)**

Completely eliminate the word "don't" from your vocabulary. Think of what you would like (or want) people to do, and say so.

***Accentuate the Positive, Eliminate the Negative* ... (Chapter 2)**

Eliminate as many negative words from your conversation, emails, texts and other communication as possible. Replace them with the positive alternative.

***Apply the 'Futureless Concept' ('I am') when planning or talking about future events* ... (Chapter 3)**

Express the future as if it's already happening. For example, express things you are going to do as "I am" rather than "I will", "I must", or "I want to".

***Use Metaphors, particularly in your written communication and 'and' in conversations* ... (Chapter 4)**

Develop metaphors to suit the situation. Use 'and' to uncover the true meaning or feeling behind what someone else is expressing when they use a metaphor.

***When feeling down, change the descriptions of your negative feelings into words that are 'quirky' and more positive (to make you smile)* ... (Chapter 5)**

Better still, use metaphors that will enable you to lighten up the negativity you may feel in a challenging or difficult situation.

***Use 'I' instead of 'you' to express an issue or concern to someone or to provide advice; avoid 'but' and replace it with 'yes, and'* ... (Chapter 7)**

- The 'I', 'you', 'we' rules:

1. "**I** have a problem/issue/concern. This is how **I** see things …"
2. "How do **YOU** see it?" or "How can **YOU** help?"
3. "What can **WE** do to work through this issue?"
- and the 'yes, and' technique:
4. Replace 'but' and 'yes, but' with 'yes, and'.

Check your tone … (Chapter 8)

Make sure your tone of voice matches the words you use and your feelings.

Learn to manage the 'process' of a conversation … (Chapter 9)
1. Open a Channel – check your location, mood, posture
2. Commit to Engage – create value for the other person – listen for feelings
3. Construct Meaning – find common ground – ask questions – "tell me more …"
4. Converge on Agreement – search for areas of agreement – ask constraints and hypotheticals
5. Evolve – what's changed – Actions? Beliefs? Ideas?
6. Act or Transact – What will happen next? Who will be told?

Framing – how to reframe your perspective and that of others … (Introduction to Part 3)

In many difficult conversations we are aiming to reframe another's perspective. So the words we choose are important. Reframe negatives into positives such as:
- expressing a *problem* as an *opportunity*
- expressing a *weakness* as a *strength*
- expressing an *impossibility* as a *distant possibility*

- expressing a *distant possibility* as a *near possibility*
- expressing *unkindness* as *lack of understanding*

Triangulate – separate the people from the issue by moving the issue to another space ... (Introduction to Part 3)

Triangulation can ease the situation when the conversation gets particularly challenging or even heated – it creates a feeling of partnership rather than competition. Triangulation can in fact re-open a channel that may have started to close up. Practise using a board, book, PC or your hands to create the apex of a triangle that you can both focus on.

Finally

As was mentioned in the introduction, using the right words not only improves the impact your language has, your understanding of others' thinking and feeling, but also has a major impact on your positivity. My challenge to you therefore is to try out some of the techniques and tips outlined and let me know the results. I'd also be very interested to hear of other techniques/tips you've found useful. You can contact me at bob@nationallearning.com.au

As the novelist Joseph Conrad said, "He who wants to persuade should put his trust not in the right argument but in the right word", so – the right words will change your life.

Happy wordsmithing!
Bob Selden

Suggested answers to the short exercises contained in Chapters 1, 2 & 7

Chapter 1: Suggested answers to 'don't' exercise

An inappropriate 'don't' statement:	An appropriate positive statement is:
• Don't drop it	Hold it carefully
• Don't walk on the grass	Walk on the footpath
• In case of fire do not use lifts (or elevators)	In case of fire use the fire exit pictured in this diagram
• Wet Paint. Don't Touch	Stay Clear, or Keep 1 metre away
• Please do not throw paper towels in toilet	Dispose of paper towels in the bin provided
• Don't even think about parking here	Keep clear at all times
• In the unlikely event of an emergency, please don't panic and follow the crew's instructions	In the unlikely event of an emergency, follow the crew's instructions
• Don't run across the road	Stop. Walk slowly.
• Don't tear that up	Keep that safe

SUGGESTED ANSWERS | DON'T – HOW USING THE RIGHT WORDS WILL CHANGE YOUR LIFE

An inappropriate 'don't' statement:	An appropriate positive statement is:
• Don't lean on doors (sign seen on sliding doors in a commuter train)	Keep clear of sliding doors until they open
• Don't make jokes about bomb threats or terrorists (sign at the check-in counter at Sydney international airport)	This sign should not appear at all. It's up to the counter staff to manage such things.
• Configuring updates – don't turn off your computer	Configuring updates – leave your computer switched on until updates are finished
• Do not discard	Store in a safe place for future use
• Don't stand on moving footway (sign seen on a very narrow moving footway a.k.a. moving walkway or travelator)	Keep walking on moving footway
• Don't hold back	Give it everything!
• Don't go near the edge	Stay on the footpath or Stay behind the line

Chapter 2: Turning negative phrases into positive

Here's the negative "self-talk" phrase	Turn these into positive "self-talk" phrases
1. What if I try and fail?	1. This is working for me
2. This is difficult …	2. Challenges are there to be overcome
3. I can't do that …	3. This is working for me
4. If only I were … I would	4. I am strong and I'm doing this well

Here's the negative "self-talk" phrase	Turn these into positive "self-talk" phrases
5. Why does this always happen?	5. This is a good opportunity to try something new
6. I never get anything right …	6. I'm doing better than that this time
7. I'm stuck in this rut …	7. I've got a very clear view of where I'm going
8. I'm such a screw-up	8. I missed that one, now I'm doing it better
9. I wish I had …	9. When I work hard, I'm getting results
10. There goes another opportunity …	10. I'm learning from this experience and am applying it at the next opportunity
11. I'll never get there …	11. It's hard and I'm making it!
12. I seem to be cursed	12. With hard work I'm succeeding
13. Why doesn't this happen for me? (or, Why does this always happen to me?)	13. I missed that one and am now looking out for the next opportunity
14. He'll / She'll never change	14. I'm influencing her to be more positive
15. My kids don't respect me	15. I'm earning the respect of my children
16. I can't lose weight	16. I'm exercising regularly
17. My boss ignores me	17. I'm getting on well with all my work colleagues
18. Why don't I ever get a break?	18. I missed that one and am now looking out for the next opportunity

Here's the negative "self-talk" phrase	Turn these into positive "self-talk" phrases
19. I have no time to exercise	19. I'm exercising for 30 minutes every day
20. I'll never get out of debt	20. Little by little I'm starting to make headway
21. He / She never listens	21. I'm using more questions to make sure my message gets through

* *Notice that while many of the negative phrases are questions, all of the suggested answers are statements expressed in the present tense as if they are now happening.*

Chapter 7: Expressions of feelings

- *You neglected to …*
- *You failed to …*
- *You overlooked (or forgot) …*

1. If someone said these to me I would feel … annoyed …

- *You claim that …*
- *You say that …*
- *You state that …*

2. If someone said these to me I would feel … angry and put down …

- *You should …*
- *You ought to …*
- *You must …*

3. If someone said these to me I would feel … childish …

- *No doubt you will ...*
- *With respect, you should ...*
- *You understand of course that ...*

4. If someone said these to me I would feel ... spoken down to ...

To change these, we could say ...

- *You neglected to ...*
- *You failed to ...*
- *You overlooked (or forgot) ...*

1. I see that the xyz has been missed ....

- *You claim that ...*
- *You say that ...*
- *You state that ...*

2. I heard xyz is that correct? ....

- *You should ...*
- *You ought to ...*
- *You must ...*

3. I'd like to see it done this way ....

- *No doubt you will ...*
- *With respect, you should ...*
- *You understand of course that ...*

4. I'd like to make sure that my message is clear ....

Acknowledgements

How The Right Words Have Changed My Life

I was fortunate to undertake my formal psychology studies in my early 30s by which time I'd had both some life and some work experiences and reached (some) maturity. One of the early writers that fascinated me was D.C. McClelland who is famous for his work on the need for achievement. However, it was his research into the impact of words on developing this drive for achievement that really grabbed my attention. For example he posited that the future a society might take could be identified and predicted by the words the society currently uses in day-to-day conversations, books (particularly children's books), stories, films, plays, cartoons and indeed the popular press.

Around that time I started working for my long-term mentor, Dennis Pratt, one of Australia's foremost organisational development consultants and author of *Aspiring to Greatness: Above and Beyond Total Quality Management*. Dennis was instrumental in fostering my interest in all things to do with motivation and has been an inspiration in my consulting work over many years. Dennis and I used to run training programs for managers teaching them how to use McClelland's theory to develop a greater need for achievement. The key underpinning in this training, was training people how to write achievement-oriented stories. And although I didn't realise it at the time, this was a good example of priming and in some cases, reframing.

In terms of this current book, I need to thank Philip Rutledge, Di Dorenzi, Peter Burleigh, Humphrey Armstrong and Louisa Busca Grisoni for their both insightful and pedantic comments on the early drafts. I'm sure the book is so much better for their input. Also to my teenage co-authors on Chapter 12, Katherine and Pippa Pryor, and their father Phil for his advice and consent.

I'm also grateful to those writers who permitted me to quote from their work, such as Spiro Zavos, Sports Journalist from the *Sydney Morning Herald* who piqued my renewed interest in the Locus of Control; Professor Marianne Schmid Mast from the Université de Lausanne whose study of the impact of words on young male drivers has long fascinated me; M.K. Chen, Associate Professor Economics, at UCLA Anderson School of Management whose ongoing work on futured languages will, I believe, have major implications for our positivity; my good friends Penny Tompkins and James Lawley who first introduced me to the importance of metaphors and the use of Clean Language; Bud Hennekes, blog owner of "A Boundless World" http://www.aboundlessworld.com/about/ for his great feedback story, and many others too numerous to name but who are catalogued in the references section.

In addition to the many other influences on my thinking, I've found the following books useful and recommend them to you:

— *Metaphors in Mind*. Lawley, J. & Tompkins, P. Developing Company Press, London 2000.
— *The Brain That Changes Itself*. Doidge, N. Penguin Group, London, 2007.
— *Words Can Change Your Brain*, Newberg, A. & Waldman, M.R. Penguin Group, New York, 2012.

— *The Man Who Lied to His Laptop.* Nass, C. Penguin Group, New York 2010.
— *Getting to Yes: Negotiating Agreement Without Giving In,* Fisher, R. & Ury, W. 2nd edition. Penguin Books 1991.
— *Drive: The Surprising Truth About What Motivates Us.* Pink, D. Penguin Group, New York, 2011.
— *Rainy Brain Sunny Brain: How to Retrain Your Brain to Overcome Pessimism and Achieve a More Positive Outlook.* Fox, E. Basic Books, 2012.

Finally I'd like to thank my number one fan, my wife Anita, whose constant encouragement makes me want to succeed at everything I do.

References

Introduction

Examples of Locus of Control & Attributional Style Test at: http://psychologytoday.tests.psychtests.com/take_test.php?idRegTest=1317, or http://www.dushkin.com/connectext/psy/ch11/survey11.mhtml, or http://www.queendom.com/tests/personality/lc_access.html

Herbert, M. (Ed.) *Research with the Locus of Control Construct, Volume 3, Extensions and limitations.* Lefcourt. Academic Press. Orlando, 1984.

Judge, T.A. & Bono, J.E. Relationship of core self-evaluations traits – self-esteem, generalized self-efficacy, locus of control, and emotional stability – with job satisfaction and job performance: A meta-analysis. *Journal of Applied Psychology*, Vol 86(1), Feb 2001, pages 80 - 92.

Reference books on communication:

— Ekman, P. *Emotions Revealed: Recognizing Faces and Feelings to Improve Communication and Emotional Life.* Henry Holt & Co. 2003.

— LeDoux, J. *The Emotional Brain: The Mysterious Underpinnings of Emotional Life.* Simon & Schuster 1998.

— Dotz, T., Hobyar T. & Sanders, S. *NLP: The Essential Guide to Neuro Linguistic Programming.* William Morris Paperbacks 2013.

Silberstein, N. Locus of Control. *Alive Australia.* May 2005.

Chapter 2

Bacal, R. Using Positive Language. *Success in Today's Workplace.* http://work911.com/articles/poslan.htm. Retrieved 21 March 2015.

REFERENCES | DON'T – HOW USING THE RIGHT WORDS WILL CHANGE YOUR LIFE

Bargh, J.A., Lee-Chai, K., Barbdollar, P.M., Gollwitzer, R. & Trötschel, R. The Automated Will: Nonconscious Activation and Pursuit of Behavioral Goals. *Journal of Personality and Social Psychology.* 2001 Dec; 81(6): pages 1014–1027.

Fox, E. *Rainy Brain Sunny Brain.* William Heinemann 2012.

Negatives. *Grammarly Handbook.* http://www.grammarly.com/handbook/sentences/negatives/. Retrieved 23 March 2015.

Newberg, A. & Waldman, M.R. *Words Can Change Your Brain.* Penguin Group 2012.

Schmid Mast, M., Sieverding, M., Esslen M., Graber, K. & Jäncke, L. Masculinity causes speeding in young men. *Accident Analysis & Prevention,* 2008; 40(2): pages 840 - 842.

Snyder, E. *Statistics on Texting & Cell Phone Use While Driving.* https://www.edgarsnyder.com/car-accident/cause-of-accident/cell-phone/cell-phone-statistics.html. Retrieved 21 March 2015.

World Health Organization. *Mobile phone use: a growing problem of driver distraction.* http://www.who.int/violence_injury_prevention/publications/road_traffic/distracted_driving_en.pdf. Retrieved 21 March 2015.

Chapter 3

Chen, M.K. Associate Professor Economics, UCLA Anderson School of Management. http://www.anderson.ucla.edu/faculty/keith.chen/. Retrieved 16 March 2015.

Chen, M.K. *The Effect of Language on Economic Behavior: Evidence from Savings Rates, Health Behaviors, and Retirement Assets.* http://www.anderson.ucla.edu/faculty/keith.chen/papers/LanguageWorkingPaper.pdf. Retrieved 16 March 2015.

Chapter 4

Geary, J. *Metaphorically Speaking.* http://www.ted.com/talks/james_geary_metaphorically_speaking?language=en. Retrieved 20 April 2015.

Gibbs, R.W. *The Cambridge Handbook of Metaphor and Thought.* Cambridge University Press, London 2008.

Grove, D. http://www.cleanlanguage.co.uk/articles/authors/7/Grove,-David. Retrieved 20 April 2015

Laceya, S., Stillaa, R. & Sathian, K. Metaphorically feeling: Comprehending textural metaphors activates somatosensory cortex. *Brain & Language,* March 2012; 120(3): pages 416 - 421.

Lakoff G. & Johnson M. *Metaphors We Live By.* University of Chicago Press 1980.

Lawley, J. & Tompkins, P. *Metaphors in Mind.* Developing Company Press, London 2000.

Sample, I. Brain scan sheds light on secret of speech, *The Guardian,* 3 Feb 2004.

The Clean Language Collection. http://www.cleanlanguage.co.uk/. Retrieved 20 April 2015.

Watkins, K.E., Paus, T., Lerch, J.P., Zijdenbos, A., Collins, D.L., Neelin, P., Taylor, J., Worsley, K.J. and Evans, A.C. Structural Asymmetries in the Human Brain: a Voxel-based Statistical Analysis of 142 MRI Scans, *Cerebral Cortex,* Volume 11, Issue 9, Sept 2001.

Chapter 5

Bargh, J.A., Professor of Psychology and Cognitive Science, Yale University. *Social Psychology Network.* Retrieved 20 April 2015.

Bargh, J. A. What have we been priming all these years? On the development, mechanisms, and ecology of nonconscious social behavior. *European Journal of Social Psychology,* (2006) 36: pages 147-168.

Briñol, P., Gascó, M. Petty, R.E. and Horcajo, J. Treating Thoughts as Material Objects Can Increase or Decrease Their Impact on Evaluation. *Psychological Science,* 12 April 2012.

Cartwright, J. *The Word is ... 'Unstucking': How changing your words can get your brain moving again.* http://www.stevenaitchison.co.uk/blog/the-word-is%E2%80%A6-unstucking-how-changing-your-words-can-get-your-brain-moving-again%E2%80%A6/ Retrieved 16 June 2015.

Ekman, P (Ed); Davidson, R. J. (Ed). The nature of emotion: Fundamental questions. *Series in affective science.* New York, NY, US: Oxford University Press. (1994) xiv: page 496.

REFERENCES | DON'T – HOW USING THE RIGHT WORDS WILL CHANGE YOUR LIFE

Kraft, T.L & Pressman, S.D. Grin and Bear It: The Influence of Manipulated Facial Expression on the Stress Response. *Psychological Science.* November 2012 Vol. 23 No. 11: pages 1372-1378.

Robbins, T. Change Your Words, Change Your Life: The Simplest Tool I Know for Immediately Transforming the Quality of Your Life. *Linkedin*, 26 Oct 2012. https://www.linkedin.com/pulse/20121026164951-101706366-change-your-words-change-your-life-the-simplest-tool-i-know-for-immediately-transforming-the-quality-of-your-life#comments-5667638207601188926. Retrieved 20 April 2015

Williams, L. E. & Bargh, J.A. Experiencing Physical Warmth Promotes Interpersonal Warmth. *Science,* 24 October 2008: Vol. 322 no. 5901: pages 606-607.

Chapter 6

Doidge, N. *The Brain That Changes Itself.* Penguin Group, London, 2007.

Kyols, K.J. *Redirecting Children's Behavior.* Parenting Press; 3rd Revised edition, January 1, 1998.

Nass, C. *The Man Who Lied to His Laptop.* The Penguin Group, 2012.

Newberg, A. & Waldman, M.R. *Words Can Change Your Brain,* Penguin Group, New York, 2012.

Mar, R.A., Oatley, J. & Peterson, J.B. Exploring the link between reading fiction and empathy: Ruling out individual differences and examining outcomes. *Communications,* 2009; 34(4): pages 407-428.

The Brain From Top to Bottom. http://thebrain.mcgill.ca/index.php. Retrieved 27 March 2015.

Slobin, D.I. *Psycholinguistics,* 2nd Ed. Scott, Foresman and Company 1971.

Chapter 7

Blakey, J. *8 Words to Avoid when Giving Feedback.* https://www.linkedin.com/pulse/8-words-avoid-when-giving-john-blakey. Retrieved 15 March 2015.

Hough, K. "Yes, But" – The Evil Twin to "Yes, And" *Huff Post*, March 23 2015.

Kington, M. I hear what you're saying but I'll ignore it. *The Independent,* October 9, 1996. http://www.independent.co.uk/voices/i-hear-what-youre-saying-but-ill-ignore-it-1357551.html. Retrieved 15 March 2015.

McDowell, S. The *'Yes, And…' Approach: Less Ego, More Openness, More Possibility. Making Things Happen.* http://99u.com/articles/7183/the-yes-and-approach-less-ego-more-openness-more-possibility. Retrieved 15 March 2015.

Seider, B.H., Hirschberger, G., Nelson, K.L. & Levenson, R.W. We can work it out: age differences in relational pronouns, physiology, and behavior in marital conflict. *Psychol Aging.* 2009 Sep; 24(3): pages 604 - 613.

Chapter 8

Atkinson, M. *Lend me your ears: All you need to know about making speeches and presentations.* Vermilion, 2004.

Cognitive Dissonance. *Simply Psychology.* http://www.simplypsychology.org/cognitive-dissonance.html. Retrieved 8 April 2015.

Grossmann, T., Vaish, A., Franz, J., Schroeder, R., Stonking, M. & Friederici, A.D. Emotional Voice Processing: Investigating the Role of Genetic Variation in the Serotonin Transporter across Development. *PLOS,* July 2013.

Hall, L.M. Blasting Away an Old NLP Myth: Meta-States in NLP Patterns Series. What carries the Most Impact in Communication? Verbal or Non-Verbal Channels? *Neuro-Semantics* at http://www.neurosemantics.com/nlp-critiques/the-7-38-55-myth retrieved 5 April 2015.

Human brain becomes tuned to voices and emotional tone of voice during infancy. *Science Daily,* 25 March 2010 at http://www.sciencedaily.com/releases/2010/03/100324121004.htm. Retrieved 9 April 2015.

Mehrabian, A. *Silent messages: Implicit communication of emotions and attitudes.* Belmont, CA: Wadsworth at http://www.kaaj.com/psych/smorder.html. Retrieved 7 April 2015.

Newberg, A. & Waldman, M.R. *Words Can Change Your Brain,* Penguin Group, New York, 2012.

Sample, I. Brain scan sheds light on secret of speech, *The Guardian* 3 Feb 2004.

Chapter 9

Clark, B. 50 Trigger Words and Phrases for Powerful Multimedia Content. *Copyblogger*, http://www.copyblogger.com/trigger-words/ retrieved 15 April 2015.

de Gelder, B., Tamietto, M., Pegna, A.J. & Van den Stock, J. Visual imagery influences brain responses to visual stimulation in bilateral cortical blindness. *ScienceDirect*, Special Issue Cortex (2014): pages 1-12.

Dubberly, H. What is conversation? How can we design for effective conversation? *ddo* at http://www.dubberly.com/articles/what-is-conversation.html. Retrieved 9 April 2015.

Fox, E. *Rainy Brain, Sunny Brain*. Arrow Books, 2013.

Garrod, S. & Pickering, M.J. Why is conversation so easy? *TRENDS in Cognitive Sciences* Vol.8 No.1 January 2004 pages 8-11.

Gibbs, R.W. *The Cambridge Handbook of Metaphor and Thought*. Cambridge University Press, London 2008.

Menenti, L., Pickering, M.J. & Garrod, S.C. Towards a neural basis of interactive alignment in conversation, *Frontiers in Human Neuroscience*. http://www.ncbi.nlm.nih.gov/pmc/articles/PMC3384290/. Retrieved 16 April 2015.

Pikiewicz, K. Submissive Listening, Therapeutic Listening and the Third Ear. *Meaningful You* in *Psychology Today* https://www.psychologytoday.com/blog/meaningful-you/201208/submissive-listening-therapeutic-listening-and-the-third-ear. Retrieved 28 April 2015.

Chapter 10

Bernstein, A.J. http://www.albernstein.com/home.htm. Retrieved 23 April 20.

Gottman, J. & Gottman, J.S. *The Gottman Institute*. http://www.gottman.com/. Retrieved 23 April 2015.

Gratz, K.L. & Roemer, L. Multidimensional Assessment of Emotion Regulation and Dysregulation: Development, Factor Structure, and Initial Validation of the Difficulties in Emotion Regulation Scale. *Journal of Psychopathology and Behavioral Assessment*. March 2004, Volume 26, Issue 1: pages 41-54.

Introduction to Part 3

Gross, J.J. Emotion regulation: Affective, cognitive, and social consequences. *Psychophysiology*, Cambridge University Press, 39 (2002): pages 281–291.

Laurent, S.M. & Myers, M.W. I know you're me, but who am I? Perspective taking and seeing the other in the self. *Journal of Experimental Social Psychology.* Volume 47, Issue 6, November 2011, Pages 1316–1319.

Chapter 11

Allen, J. P., Chango, J., Szwedo, D. E., Schad, M. M., & Marston, E. G. Predictors of susceptibility to peer influence regarding substance use in adolescence. *Child Development*, 2012. 83(1): pages 337-350.

Giedd, J. N. Development of the human corpus callosum during childhood and adolescence: A longitudinal MRI study. *Progress in Neuro-Psychopharmacology & Biological Psychiatry.* 1999. 23: pages 571-588.

Chapter 12

http://kidshealth.org/teen/your_mind/families/talk_to_parents.html#. By D'Arcy Lyness, Reviewed (2015) Retrieved 1 June 2015.

Chapter 13

Depp, C.A., Glatt, S.J. & Jeste, D.V. (2007). Recent advances in research on successful or healthy ageing. *Current Psychiatry Reports* (2007) 9 (1): pages 7–13.

Vaidya, A. Seniors set in their ways? *Medill Reports Chicago*, 19 Jan 2012 http://newsarchive.medill.northwestern.edu/chicago/news-198874.html. Retrieved 28 April 2015.

Chapter 14

Ginott, H. G. *Between Parent And Child*. Macmillan, New York 1965.

Globis Mediation Group. How to Reduce Stress in the Workplace. *People Management Magazine*, 10 Aug 2006. Retrieved 21 May 2015.

Hennekes, B. *A Boundless World* http://www.aboundlessworld.com/about/ Retrieved 21 May 2015.

Nass, C. *The Man Who Lied to His Laptop*. Penguin Group, New York 2010.

O'Keeffe, A. Why The Feedback Sandwich Doesn't Work. *The National Learning Institute*. www.nationallearning.com.au. Retrieved 21 May 2015.

Stone, D. & Heen, S. *Thanks for the Feedback: The Science and Art of Receiving Feedback Well*. Viking, 2014.

Chapter 15

Ames, D. Pushing Up to a Point. The Psychology of Interpersonal Assertiveness. In Forgas, J., Kruglanski, A. & Williams, K. (Eds.), *Social conflict and aggression*. New York, NY: Psychology Press, 2011.

Chapter 16

Barber, C. *A short speech – create a 3 minute speech that rocks*. October 28, 2012. http://vividmethod.com/a-short-speech-create-a-3-minute-speech-that-rocks/. Retrieved 15 April 2015.

Naidoo, J.J. & Lord, R.G. Speech imagery and perceptions of charisma: The mediating role of positive affect. *Leadership Quarterly*, 2008 June; 19(3): pages 283-296.

Stocchetti, M. & Kukkonen, K. *Images in use: Towards the critical analysis of visual communication*. John Benjamins Publishing, 2011.

Chapter 17

Fisher, R. & Ury, W. *Getting to Yes: Negotiating Agreement Without Giving In* 2nd edition. Penguin Books 1991.

Chapter 18

Barth, F.D. 5 Steps for Dealing With Someone Who Won't Stop Talking. *Psychology Today*, 22 April 2015. https://www.psychologytoday.com/blog/the-couch/201204/5-steps-dealing-someone-who-wont-stop-talking. Retrieved 22 June 2015.

Bernstein, E. Why Verbal Tee-Ups Like 'To Be Honest' Often Signal Insincerity. *The Wall Street Journal* 20 Jan 2014. Retrieved 13 July 2015.

Food, Fun and Conversation: 1,2,3,4 weeks to better family dinners. *The Family Dinner Project*. http://thefamilydinnerproject.org/4week-program/support/conversation-stoppers/ Retrieved 23 June 2015.

Hancock, B. & Rubin, B.A. Influence of Communication Partner's Gender on Language. *Journal of Language and Social Psychology*, 11 May 2014.

McClish, M. *Unique Words: "Actually" Detecting Deception Using Statement Analysis.* http://www.blifaloo.com/info/actually-statement-analysis.php. Retrieved 23 June 2015.

Newman, M.L., Pennebaker, J.W. & Berry, D.S. Lying Words: Predicting Deception From Linguistic Styles. *Personality and Social Psychology Bulletin* (2003) 29 (5), 665 - 675.

Index

3 Magic tricks for managing emotional outbursts 131–3, 134
3 Smart Cubes 26
4 steps for initiating a conversation 128–30, 134
21-day plan 13

Act or Transact 96–7, 98, 106, 107, 110
 parent and young adult conversations 141–2
 speeches/presentations, in 204
advice, giving 167–70 *see also* feedback
 assumptions, testing 169
 brainstorming 170
 conversation process, managing 170
 expanding the frame of reference 169–70
 guidelines 168–70
 permission, asking 168
 regularity of 168–9
 sounding board, acting as 169
 techniques to avoid 171–2
 words to avoid 170–1
advice, listening to 172–4
aggressive communicators 125
ageing parent
 agreement, obtaining 155
 conversation with 153–63
 disagreeing with 160
 future, discussions regarding 157–8
 keeping the conversation on track 159
 managing the conversation with 157–8
 objections to conversation 159–60
 phrases to avoid 161–2
 planning for 'that' conversation 155–6
 relationship with 154–5
 similar issues, raising 156–7
 words to avoid 161–2
'although', using 78
 advice, giving 170
'and'
 questions starting with 37–9, 43, 229
 replacing 'but' 49–50, 54–5, 115
argument, defusing an 229–30
assertive communicators 125–8
assertiveness xiv, 125–7, 150, 159–60, 218
 aggressiveness, distinguished 179
 continuum 186–8
 defining 178, 179
 examples 182–6
 guidelines 186
 logic, avoiding 186, 218
 logic, listening to 188
 overbearing, reducing 188
 personal outcomes, impact on 182, 184
 practising 187–8
 relationships, impact on 180–1, 218
 self-reflection 179–80
 style, identifying your natural 179–82
 words we use 178–9
Atkinson, Max 89

Bach-y-Rita, Paul 58

Barber, Cam 199
Bargh, John 16, 17, 46, 47
Bath, Diane 218
behaviour
    influencing others' 3–9
    words we use regularly and 15–23
Bernstein, Dr Albert 131, 132
Blakey, John 67, 69
brain
    language regions 58
    metaphors, impact of 36–7, 48
    positive and negative words 2, 56–62
    thalamic changes *see* thalamic changes
    'you' conversations 69
'but', using 64, 77–9, 115, 229
    advice, giving 170

Cartright, Joshua 48
Chen, Associate Professor M. Keith 27–30
    TED talk 33
Clark, Brian 112
Clean Language 2, 37–9, 44, 80, 101, 105
Clinton, Hilary 191
coaches, sporting ix–xi
    positive instructions 4–5
cognitive reappraisal 119
Commit to Engage 95, 98, 100–4, 107, 109
    ageing parents, conversations with 159
    parent and young adult conversations 140
    speeches/presentations, in 204
    spouse/partner conversations 128, 129
communication xiv, 232
    Clean Language *see* Clean Language
    conversations *see* conversations
    types of communicators 124–6
    visual xii, 3, 35
communicators 124–6

aggressive 125
assertive 125–8
passive 125
passive/aggressive 125
Conrad, Joseph 235
Construct Meaning 96, 98, 104–5, 107, 109
    ageing parents, conversations with 159
    parent and young adult conversations 140
    speeches/presentations, in 204
    spouse/partner conversations 128, 129
Converge on Agreement 96, 98, 105–6, 107, 110
    ageing parents, conversations with 159
    parent and young adult conversations 140–1
    speeches/presentations, in 204
    spouse/partner conversations 128, 129
conversation deepeners 228
conversation stoppers 223–5, 227
    examples 225–7
conversations 93–4, 217–31
    Act or Transact 96–7, 98, 106, 107, 110, 141–2, 204
    body language 120
    challenges to fluidity 98
    Commit to Engage 95, 98, 100–4, 107, 109, 128, 129, 140, 159, 204
    Construct Meaning 96, 98, 104–5, 107, 109, 128, 129, 140, 159, 204
    content 97
    Converge on Agreement 96, 98, 105–6, 107, 110, 128, 129, 140–1, 159, 204
    difficult 64, 65–84, 124, 133–4
    Evolve 96, 98, 106, 107, 110, 141, 204
    'I' perspective 122–3
    managing 64, 93–108, 112–13, 128–30

Open a Channel 95, 98, 100, 107, 109, 120, 128, 129, 140, 159, 204
participants, tasks of 94–7
practising conversation process management 108–12
process 97, 107–8, 115, 127, 234
triangulation 120–2
yourself, with 230–1
criticism 66–8, 74, 77–9, 171, 174–5
feedback and *see* feedback
teenage hyper sensitivity 137, 140
cultural potholes 196

dependency 153
discussion space 100
Doidge, Norman 58
Donne, John 41
'don't'
eliminating xi–xii, 5, 10–14, 61, 114, 233
rewriting statements 10–11
signs using 6–7
speeches/presentations, in 193
double processing 3–4
driving
impact of words on 15–16
Dubberly, Hugh 94, 95

Eckman, Paul 48
ego 166
embodied cognition 46, 52
emotional contagion 99–100
emotions *see* feelings
empty cup (Zen) xv
Evolve 96, 98, 106, 107, 110
parent and young adult conversations 141
speeches/presentations, in 204
exercises
'and', changing 'but' to 54–5
answers to 236–40
changing how you feel 52–5
changing your language 12–14, 24–5

Constraints Questions, using 112
'facts' and 'feelings', distinguishing 111–12
Hypothetical Questions, using 112
improving your tone 91–2
'ing' suffix, using 53–4
merging the present and future 32–3
metaphors, using 42–3, 52–5
practising Conversation Process Management 108–11
words and metaphors to change feelings, using 52–5
'you' conversations 71–2
expression of genes 56
external focus x–xi

facial expressions 85–9
mirroring 99
facts
feelings, distinguished 101–2, 111–12
listening to 101–4
spouse/partner conversations 127
feedback, giving 67–8, 101, 164–72
advice *see* advice
criticism *see* criticism
favourable 167–70
'feedback sandwich' 171–2
future-oriented words, using 167–8
praise *see* praise
reframing 167–8
techniques to avoid 171–2
tone of voice 168
words to avoid 170–1
feedback, receiving 172–4
feelings (emotions)
behaviour, focusing on 119
calm, remaining 130, 131
criticism, responding to 165
depowering 229
emotional trigger words 112–13
exercises 52–5
explaining your 127
facts, distinguished 101–2, 111–12

identifying 88–9
listening to 101–4
reframing and 119
'think' and 'feel', comparison 102–3
words influencing 2, 45–8, 55, 61
fiction, reading 57–8, 59
Fisher, Roger 212
flattery 176
football xi–xii
referees 8–9
Ford, Henry 119
Fox, Professor Elaine 26
framing *see* reframing
functional magnetic resonance imaging (fMRI) 57–8, 59
future tense languages (FTL)
hard 28–30
soft 28, 29
Futureless Concept 2, 30–1, 33, 61, 114, 233
action expressed as already happening 31
exercises 32–3

Garrod, Simon 98
Gibbs, Raymond W. 35, 36, 99
Ginott, Haim G. 175
Gollwitzer, Peter 16, 17
Gottman, Dr John 127, 129
Gottman, Dr Julie 127
Gross, James J. 119
Grossmann, Dr Tobias 90
Grove, David 37

Hancock, Adrienne 217
Hennekes, Bud 165–7, 174
honesty 103, 124, 126, 137, 149, 166, 167, 195, 214–15, 223–7
hormones, stress-producing 19
hot-desking 5–6
'however', using 78
advice, giving 170

'I' message 68–70, 115, 229
changing 'you' into 'I' 70–2
difficult conversations and 'you' 72–3
exceptions 74–5
guidelines for using 73–4
manipulative use of 72–3
rules for using 76–7, 80, 82–4, 233–4
speeches/presentations, in 204
'we', using 75–7
'I' perspective 122–3
advantages 123
assertiveness *see* assertiveness
conversations with ageing parents 157
spouse/partner conversations 127, 130
imagery 190–2, 197, 199
personal 193
'ing' suffix 48–9
exercise 53–4
interactive alignment 99
internal focus x–xi
Isaacson, Walter 217

Johnson, Dr C.E. 90
Johnson, Martin 36

King, Martin Luther Jr 197–9
Kington, Miles 81

Lakoff, George 36
language, changing your
exercises 12–14
rewriting statements 10–11
language regions of the brain 58
Lawley, James 36, 37, 38
listening 229
Commit to Engage *see* Commit to Engage
facts, to 101
feelings, to 101
reflective 80–2, 101

Locus of Control x–xi, 17
    changing your xi–xii
logic
    assertiveness and 186, 188, 218
    speeches/presentations, in 191–2, 193
Lord, Robert G. 190, 192

McCain, John 191–2
magnetic resonance imaging (MRI) 57–8, 59
'may' and 'can', distinguished 220–1
Mehrabian, Professor Albert 88
metaphors 34–41, 43–4, 61, 105, 114–15, 233
    brain, impact on 36–7, 48
    changing how you feel 51–5
    cultural specificity 39
    definition 35
    examples 39–40
    exercises 42–3, 52–5
    influencing difficult people through 42
    interpreting 198–9
    limitations 40
    power of 35–6, 45, 48
    speeches/presentations, in 190–1, 193, 194–9
    television and movies, from 42
    visual communication 35
Mind Tools 26
mirroring 99
mother tongue 1, 27
movement, internal sense of 48–9

Naidoo, James J. 190, 192
Nass, Clifford 62, 176
needs 208–10
    determining 210–11
    wants, distinguished 209, 214
negation 18, 221
    common stoppers 222–7
negative framing 118
negative outlook x
    conversations with yourself 231

negative phrases 19–20, 60
    eliminating 24, 233
    self-talk 20–3
negative signage 6–7, 8
negative words 18–19, 62
    brain power, and 2, 56–62
    cognitive complexity 59–60
    eliminating 61, 114, 233
    impact 19, 26
    rewriting statements 10–11
negotiation 206–16
    asking for more than required 208–11
    being prepared 207
    concessions, making 208, 212–13
    error/omission, admitting 208, 214–15
    negative response, receiving a 208, 211–12
    options, developing 211–12
    quiz 208–15
    tips 215–16
    win/win results 208, 213–14
neurotransmitters 19
New Business Pack 29
New Year's resolutions 32
Newberg, Andrew 19
'No Man is an Island' 41

Obama, Barack 191, 192
O'Keeffe, Andrew 172
Open a Channel 95, 98, 100, 107, 109, 120
    ageing parents, conversations with 159
    parent and young adult conversations 140
    speeches/presentations, in 204
    spouse/partner conversations 128, 129
opening statements, practising 130

parent conversations
    ageing parent, conversation with 153–63

listening to young adults 146
   self-reflection 137–8
   timing 138–9, 154
   young adult, with 135–44
partner to partner conversations 124–8, 133–4
   managing difficult 128–31
   when your partner starts 131–3
passive communicators 125
passive/aggressive communicators 125
Pennebaker, James W. 224
performatives 224, 227
personal language
   impact of 1, 27–30
physical actions, performing 51
Pickering, Martin 98
positive framing 118–19
positive instructions 4, 12–13
positive outlook x, 15, 21, 231
   building blocks 1
   using words to intensify feelings 48–50
positive phrases 60, 62
   cognitive complexity 59–60
   emails and text messages 24
   self-talk 22–3
positive signage 7–8
positive words
   brain power, and 2, 56–62
   rewriting statements 10–11
   using 26, 114
praise, giving 74, 174–5 *see also* feedback
   adults, to 176–7
   children, to 175–6
   descriptive praise 176
   motivation and 175, 176
   performance, influencing 177
presentations 190–205
   choosing the words 193–6
   structuring 199–203
priming 1, 25, 46, 121
   examples 47
problem statements
   eliminating 24–5
prosody 91
Psychology Today 26
'push' energy 189, 218

qualifiers 224–7
questions
   'and', starting with 37–9, 43, 229
   Constraints Questions 105, 112
   constructing meaning 104–5
   conversation stoppers (examples) 225–7
   Hypothetical Questions 105, 112
   non-questions, handling 221–2
   rational, asking 131–3
quirky words 61, 115, 233

reciprocity 214
referees 8–9
reflective listening 80–2, 101
   phrases 81–2
reframing 93, 117–20, 234–5
   examples 118
   feedback 167–8
   negative 118
   positive 118–19
   teenagers, conversations with 139
   timing 119
resource dilemma game 16–17
rhetoric 190, 191, 197, 204
Robbins, Tony 45–6, 50
Rotter, Julian x
rowing 4–5
Rubin, Benjamin 217

Sample, Ian 90
Sanchez, Julia 62
saving money 27–30
Schmid Mast, Professor Marianne 16
Schmidt, Eric 217
Schrauf, Robert 62
Seider, Benjamin 76
self-talk
   negative *see* negative phrases
   positive *see* positive phrases
senses 58
signpost language 199–203
sincerity 80–1, 84, 101, 130, 175
small business 29
Smith, Megan 217
sorry, saying 215, 230

speeches 190–205
    choosing the words 193–6
    structuring 199–203
spouse to spouse conversations 124–8, 133–4
    managing difficult 128–31
    when your partner starts 131–3
Stone, Douglas 173
structure of book xii–xv
summarising 229–30
swapping sides 230

talking over the top 227
    countering 217–21
teenagers *see* young adults
thalamic changes
    perceptions of reality, and 57
    'you' conversations 69
thoughts
    'think' and 'feel', comparison 102–3
    writing down 51–2
Tomkins, Penny 36, 37, 38
tone of voice 64, 85–91, 92, 115, 229, 234
    advice, giving 168
    improving your 91–2
Transderivational Morphology 48–9
triangulation 120–2, 188, 230, 235
    definition (geometry) 120
    examples 121–2
    teenagers, conversations with 139
trust 87, 103, 110, 113, 149, 224

Ury, William 212

voice, tone of *see* tone of voice

Waldman, Mark 19
wants
    needs, distinguished 209, 214
    negotiation, in 208

warmth 47
'we' conversations 75–7
    rules for 76–7, 80
Williams, Judith 217
Williams, Lawrence 47
word exclamations, enriching 222
word pictures, building resonating 190–1

'yes, and' 79, 80, 101
    advice, giving 170
    suggestions for practising 82–4
'yes, but' 64, 77–9, 115, 229
    advice, giving 170
'you' conversations 65–8, 229
    assertiveness and aggressiveness, distinguishing 179
    blame or criticism, inferring 66–7
    brain, and the 69
    changing 'you' into 'I' 70–2
    difficult situations, in 72–3
    future tense 74
    present tense 74–5
    rules for 76–7, 80, 233–4
    'we', using 75–7
young adults
    advice, seeking 147
    brain development 135–6
    challenges 144
    characteristics 136–7
    engaging with 139–42
    feelings, identifying 148
    knowing what you want from a conversation 146–8
    listen, asking parents to 146
    mistakes, talking about 147–8
    opening conversations with 136–9
    parent conversations with 135–44
    permission, seeking 146
    questions from 143
    support, seeking 146
    talking to parents 145–52
    timing of conversations 138–9, 149
    tips for 149–51

Zavos, Spiro ix

 Bob Selden is the author of 'What To Do When You Become The Boss: How new managers become successful managers'. It's sold over 55,000 copies and been published in four languages. This new book 'Don't' now pinnacles his life-time experience and research into how words impact our behaviour and ultimately make us 'who we are'.

www.ingramcontent.com/pod-product-compliance
Lightning Source LLC
Chambersburg PA
CBHW020317010526
44107CB00054B/1880